# Take Me or Leave Me

A Memoir

By Dr. Lauren Bridges

This book is the story of part of my life as I remember it. Nothing is made up. Most names are changed out of consideration for others.

It Mattered to Me


The day you gave me up…

…it mattered to me.

The day you said, "I don't make enough money to keep you."

…it mattered to me.

The day you stopped fighting for me

…it mattered to me.

The day you said it was my fault…

…it mattered to me.

The day you replaced me…

…it mattered to me.

The day you forgot about me…

…it mattered to me.

The day you injured my soul.…

…it mattered to me.

Connection is why we are here. We are hardwired to connect with others; it's what gives purpose and meaning to our lives and without it there is suffering.
**Brene Brown**


When something happens, we have three choices. We can either let it define us, let it destroy us, or we can let it strengthen us.
**Dr. Seuss**

# Acknowledgements

This book is dedicated to my husband, Dr. Drew Bridges. He encouraged and guided me from the initial idea, through the several years of work, to completion.
Many thanks to my writing group: Gale, Christy, Robin, and Drew.

# Table of Contents


Chapter 1: The Surprise Visitor ................................................................ 1

Chapter 2: The Tragic Separation ............................................................ 8

Chapter 3: Don't Cry Over Spilled Milk ................................................ 11

Chapter 4: Moving On .............................................................................. 17

Chapter 5: Reunited with Richard .......................................................... 21

Chapter 6: Opportunity Knocks .............................................................. 27

Chapter 7: The Audition ........................................................................... 33

Chapter 8: Another Roll of the Dice ....................................................... 38

Chapter 9: A Sleepless Night ................................................................... 43

Chapter 10: Sunday Blues ......................................................................... 47

Chapter 11: Two's Company and Three's a Crowd ............................... 52

Chapter 12: Some Changes Ain't that Bad ............................................. 56

Chapter 13: "The Grass May be Greener on the Other Side." ............. 61

Chapter 14: Home Sweet Home ............................................................... 64

Chapter 15: Now Why Am I Here? .......................................................... 67

Chapter 16: Thorns in My Crown ........................................................... 72

Chapter 17: Bittersweet Victory .............................................................. 77

Chapter 18: Heading for Trouble ............................................................ 81

Chapter 19: It's Better to Give Than to Receive ................................... 86

Chapter 20: Those Evil Eyes .................................................................... 90

Chapter 21: You Can't Judge a Book by Its Cover ................................... 94

Chapter 22: A Surprise Summer ................................................................. 97

Chapter 23: Growing Up ............................................................................ 101

Chapter 24: I'm in the Driver's Seat ........................................................ 106

Chapter 25: You Get What You Pay For ................................................. 112

Chapter 26: The End is in Sight ............................................................... 117

Chapter 27: Things are Looking Up ........................................................ 121

Chapter 28: No Looking Back ................................................................... 128

Chapter 29: A Night to Remember ........................................................... 134

Chapter 30: It's Time for Me to Go .......................................................... 140

# Chapter 1
# The Surprise Visitor

Memories of a childhood. Where do they begin? Do they ever end? For me, they began the summer of 1967 in Fayetteville, North Carolina. As a young child, I recall my family moving from house to house, dodging landlords, bill collectors and even the milk man. These moves eventually became routine and in an odd way, even exciting for me and my four brothers. During one of our many moves I decided to save time and didn't bother to unpack my clothes and childhood treasures, as I knew the next move was only a matter of time.

My father was considered the breadwinner in our family, while my mother was our caretaker. I was the second oldest of the children. This partnership between my parents seemed to work reasonably well until my father's drinking became unmanageable. I realized my dad had a serious problem when I was 7 years old. His drinking often left us without food and even electricity for several days. It was also around that time, I became more like the caretaker, as my mom became more and more depressed. In many ways, I became the one charge, as I cooked, cleaned, and bathed my three younger brothers.

The most excitement of the summer was about the ice cream truck that would roll through our neighborhood streets. All kids hoped their parents would buy them ice-cream, sodas, hot dogs, and candy. We were lucky to visit the ice-cream man maybe three times over the course of the summer.

The school that I attended was Pauline Jones Elementary School. One memory that I have about the school was constantly being teased by my classmates for being the "teacher's pet." In those early elementary years, my relationships with teachers were nurturing and provided me with reassurance and guidance.

Many of my teachers recognized my strong determination and efforts to study hard. At the end of my second grade, I received an unexpected classroom award. The award was for my perfect attendance and outstanding grades. I have memories of finishing up second grade with a bang. Looking back, I'm amazed that I received perfect attendance. My mother was very dependent upon me and on her bad days would cry when I left for school. I never understood why she cried, but in time it became more and more obvious. She became very depressed and relied on me to run the house and care for my brothers. Many days I would try to fake my own illness, as a way to stay home to care for her. But she somehow managed to pull it together and send me off to school.

The neighborhood that we lived in that summer was known as the "poor section" of town. There was no community pool, club house or places to hang out. The meeting place for kids was in the streets. My mother always disapproved of us hanging out in the streets. But it was all we had. We would usually sneak out and play with the neighborhood kids.

We knew our mother never left the couch during the day. We were generally safe to enjoy our time playing kick ball, tag, and dodge ball with the other neighborhood kids.

One day, my dad drove by and caught us playing in the street and yelled, "Get out of the street now!" I quickly rounded up my three younger brothers and dashed home to find him sitting in his car waiting for us. It was disappointing to find that my dad was still sitting in his car and had not gone inside to be with our mom. That was the day I learned dad was never going back inside our house to check on mom, or on us kids for that matter. Dad told us that he would be living in a different house but would still be taking care of us. I didn't believe him, as we were already two months behind on the rent. That was the last time my dad ever visited us.

As he drove away, I wanted to run after him and tell him that I hated him. But at the same time, my mind raced back to taking care of mom and paying the rent.

I never told mom about Dad's visit on that day. This news would only add to her sadness. I bribed my brothers that afternoon with an ice-cream cone to keep Dad's visit a secret. I was able to trade one of my favorite dolls with a neighborhood girl in exchange for twenty-five cents so that I was able to keep my promise to my brothers.

It was difficult for me to accept that my dad was not a part of our family, but in other ways, the separation helped me avoid my anger and resentment towards him. However, that changed the day my mother received an eviction notice for being three months behind on our rent. Mother's reaction to the news was amazingly calm and accepting. I became very angry with her and shouted, "Are you just going to keep laying there on that couch? Why don't you stand up to him?" Mom only stared and resumed her position on the couch.

This became another defining moment for me as a young child, taking hold of yet another responsibility. I woke up earlier than usual the next morning and got a jump start on my chores. I had a private pow-pow with my brothers outside. I told them I had to run an important errand but would be back soon. Once again, I had to use another ice-cream bribe. I really didn't know how I was going to fulfill this promise. I couldn't fathom parting with my last doll to secure enough money to buy more ice cream.

My thoughts quickly left the ice-cream bribe as I raced out the door to accomplish my errand. It was critical that once out the door, I walk as fast as possible to get away from the other neighborhood kids. The last thing that I needed was for them to follow me. Once I turned the corner, I slowed down which helped me catch my breath.

This errand that I told my brothers about was a two mile walk to my dad's job. I needed to confront him for the 3 months of back rent. I remember being afraid during my two mile walk alone. I knew I would be traveling through segments of some really rough parts of town. My mind was spinning. What if someone tried to hurt me or kidnap me? I put my fear aside to concentrate on finishing my journey.

Dad worked as a manager at Hardees and despite his battle with alcoholism had been able to keep this job for many years. Back in the 60's, fast-food restaurants were set up for customers to walk up to a window and place their orders. I stepped up to the window and asked to speak to the manager.

I was not taken very seriously. The cashier asked me to step aside because paying customers came first. My patience and kindness for being ignored eventually ran out. I jumped in front of a customer and said, "Look, I need to see my dad, Donald Beale, now!" It took only seconds before my dad appeared from outside the back of the building. Before he could utter a word, I said, "We need to have three months of rent money now. I'm not leaving here without it."

Looking surprised and speechless, my dad quickly led me behind the building and said, "How did you get here?" I replied in a rather sassy way, "Why would you care? If you must know, I walked all the way here and I'm proud of it."

My dad called the landlord while I was there and the two of them reached an agreement that stopped the eviction. My dad then insisted on driving me back home. My pride and stubbornness made me refuse his offer. I told him I wanted to go in a taxicab. With some reluctance, he agreed by giving me $5.00 to cover the fare.

When I arrived home, I was eagerly greeted by brothers with their demands of "we want our ice-cream cones today." Luckily for me, I had one dollar left over from my cab fare and was able to buy their ice-cream treats. I even treated myself that day to my own ice-cream cone. I deserved it. Surprisingly, dad kept his word, and our rent was paid. Once again, we could breathe and not have to dodge the landlord. With summer coming to an end, I felt a sense of peace. I knew that school would be starting soon and that meant an escape, as well as social opportunities for me.

One week before school was scheduled to start, my brothers got into trouble with one of our neighbors. Apparently, my middle brother, while running to get his ball that rolled into the neighbor's yard, stepped on her newly planted flowers.

This neighbor never approved of our family moving in next door and immediately placed signs in her yard saying, "No kids allowed on grass." We were told by other kids and even their parents that we were not liked by this woman with the green grass.

There was once a rumor circulating around the neighborhood that she had contacted a local church about investigating our family for suspicions that we were not receiving parental supervision. Needless to say, this was a neighbor who we tried to stay clear of. However, it may have been too late the day my brother's ball rolled into her yard.

* * *

The last official day of summer vacation finally came. The first day of school always brought about excitement. A lot of kids will show up wearing a new outfit, have school supplies and a special lunch box. I never had these luxuries. For me, having clean clothes, a new pencil and writing paper was the best we had. My younger brothers never complained about our family being poor. Being the only girl and sister to my brothers, I made sure they were clean and helped with their homework assignments. This routine would be the same for the new school year.

A few things would be different this school year, as our dad would not be around to help out with my brothers. His absence would place additional responsibilities for me.

I made the decision to leave a little early for school on our first day back. This extra time would help me in getting my brothers to school on time as well as prepare our mother for being alone until the late afternoon.

Before we made it out the door, we were distracted by a loud knocking outside of the door. I was startled and wondered who could be at our door so early in the morning. It hit me that it was probably a neighborhood kid wanting to walk with us to school. I quickly answered the door and standing outside was a tall, thin women with an unfriendly look on her face. She asked if my mother was home. I paused for a moment and asked if she would wait outside.

I remember the annoyed look on her face. I ran back inside to tell my mother about this strange visitor. She told me to let her in. Before I could get back to the door, I was surprised to see that the woman had let herself in. I lost control of my tongue and blurted out, "Who are you and what do you want from us?" She ignored me and turned towards my mother. Surprisingly, my mother spoke up and said to this strange visitor, "No it's okay. My girl can stay."

The woman pretended that she didn't hear my mother and continued to motion for me to go into another room. My mom, once again, reminded the women that I could stay in the room while they talked. It was at that time she told us she was a social worker and that she needed to check on our family.

She continued by informing my mom that she needed to ask a few questions and to verify that there was food in the house. Before I was able to interrupt, she turned to my mom and asked, "What exactly is wrong with you?" Without hesitation, I fired back, "Listen Mrs. Social

Worker, my mom is fine and doesn't need your help. I have everything under control so you can leave. Besides, I need to leave soon, as today is the first day of school. So, hurry up and finish your questions, so I can get my brothers to school."

The social worker continued asking questions. "Mrs. Joan, what exactly is wrong with you?" It became clear that this lady wasn't in any hurry to leave our house. Before the social worker was able to get out any more questions, I blurted out, "Well what do you think is wrong with her? I'll tell you what's wrong with her. It's you!" I continued by saying "My mother has been sick for who knows how long, but I am taking care of her just fine." If we need your help, we will call you later.

I was quickly interrupted by my mother, as she, in a soft -spoken voice, attempted to describe how she had been struggling with sadness and feelings of hopelessness. At the same time, my mother hinted at the fact that she might need to go to the hospital for some help. My heart sank. The worker continued to take over and replied back to my mom, "So that explains why you haven't been taking care of your children."

I couldn't believe what I was hearing from this lady. "Listen, Mrs. Social worker, we are just fine, so why don't you just leave? I told you that I needed to take my brothers to school. We are already late." It started to become clear that this lady was not leaving.

"Mrs. Joan, I think we need to get you some help. You mentioned the hospital and I agree that going there is just what you need. The social worker turned back to me and said, "Now you children don't need to worry. I have a place for you to go."

"We're not going anywhere but school. I can help my mom with getting to the hospital." "Honey that is not your job. What I need for you to do is pack up your clothes. I will be taking you to a children's home,"

"A children's home, what exactly is a children's home?" It wasn't much longer before I knew I was fighting a losing battle.

As things continued to fall apart, it was also becoming clear that my brothers and I would be taken away. I knew that my younger brothers were confused and scared so I decided to focus on them and less on the social worker. It was important to hold it together for them.

The social worker reinforced that we needed to get our belongings packed up so she could drive us to our new home. I decided to stop arguing with the social worker, as my brothers needed me more. Once our clothes were packed, I led my brothers back into the living room to say good-bye to our mom. I knew it was no good to linger. Rather it was best that I got my brothers loaded up in the car to avoid any further pain and confusion. At the last minute, I turned back towards my mom and blew her a kiss and walked out the door.

# Chapter 2
# The Tragic Separation

Leaving my mother behind on that hot, torrid summer day was painful, as was the endless ride to the Emergency Children's Home. This home was more like a "holding cell" for unwanted children. I will never forget the car ride, as I felt like I was being punished for something I had never done. There were moments when I wrestled with thoughts of jumping out of the car, running into the woods, and hiding for days, months or even years. These thoughts were quickly interrupted by outbursts of loud crying and sighs from my one-year-old brother. This seemed to be his way of letting it be known he was angry and afraid.

There was one intense moment when all three of my brothers began to cry and it was at that same time the bossy social worker shouted, "Quiet them down." This left me feeling incredibly overwhelmed and a failure, unable to better handle this situation. In so many ways, I did feel like giving up. I felt helpless and knew there was very little I could do, at least for now.

This early childhood experience became a pivotal one. It set the stage for me to hide my true feelings and emotions. At the time, I remained determined to be strong throughout the car ride to the overnight Emergency Home.

As a young child, my grandmother made it known that I was the most "stubborn" child she had ever known. The truth is, I learned how to be tough and brave by following in her footsteps. The silence in the car weighed on me. I shouted out to the Social Worker calling her "one mean and pitiful lady" for treating me and my brothers like dirt. I even went a step further to call the social worker a "bully" and told her that she reminded me of an old classmate who beat me up and stole my ten-cent lunch money.

As I was about to throw another verbal attack, I heard her bark "O.k. get your bags together, we are about to pull into the parking lot." Upon surviving the worst car trip of my life, I felt the old rusty four-door station wagon at last come to a slow creaking stop. Overcome by curiosity, I could not blurt out any more verbal attacks but was rather drawn to the overgrown lawn surrounding a small cinder block house. The first thing that popped into my mind was whether they would make me cut the grass as a punishment or a chore for being given a home.

Before I could think any more about cutting the grass, a short, pudgy woman who was carrying a notebook in one hand and an Orange Crush soda in the other came out to the car. This lady did not look happy to see us and I knew that meant trouble. The conversation between this women and Social Worker was not friendly. I remember hearing her ask, "How many children did you bring me? How many nights will they be staying?"

*Wow, what a greeting*, I mumbled under my breath. My brothers, who had managed to fall asleep during the car ride, were slowly beginning to wake. We were commanded to get our paper bags out of the car and follow the woman into the house.

I remember feeling like a prisoner; no one was interested in even knowing our names. In my heart, I knew that this place was going to be a nightmare. Sleeping arrangements for that evening proved my point. My brothers and I were led to a small bedroom that was probably the size of a large walk-in closet with sparse furnishings. I found it odd that we were never introduced and did not know this lady's name. The woman in charge quickly made it known to the social worker that the large walk-in closet was the best thing she had to offer for sleeping.

The social worker quickly chimed in by saying, "That will be just fine. These children will only be staying for a night or so. I'm sure the children will sleep well whether it's on the floor or a small bed."

I could not believe what this Social Worker said. *Who does she think she is? How would she like to sleep on some stranger's floor?* At that point in time, I had heard enough and abruptly shouted out, "my brothers and I will be just fine." The social worker turned away and made a quick exit out the front door without even a good-bye. I remember thinking that I never wanted to see this woman again.

The night was rather late and by now my youngest brother had awakened in a strange place. His loud outburst of crying was evidence that he was in unfamiliar territory. Once safely inside the bedroom, I quickly closed the door and wrapped my arms around my brother to help calm him down. By some miracle, we eventually fell asleep that night. It was a restless night, as I found myself waking up throughout the night to check on my brothers.

Daybreak finally arrived and I remember waking up to the tooting horn of an automobile. I found it odd that we had not been called for breakfast. Shortly thereafter there was a knock at the door followed by orders that we would be leaving in 30 minutes for a new home. We were instructed to get dressed and report to the kitchen for a bowl of cereal before leaving. Upon finishing our small bowl of corn flakes and glass of water, we were told to collect our bags and sit on the front porch until our ride showed up.

While passing time away, I attempted to distract my younger brothers by reading a book that I managed to pack in my bag before leaving our home. This book, *Little Red Riding Hood,* had always been one of my brother's favorite books. The story was interrupted by the squeaking sound of a car rushing into the driveway. With very little notice, a tall, thin, dark-skinned woman approached the porch and ordered that my brothers quickly get into her car. I was told to wait for another car. It was still unclear where I would be going.

I was given no information except I found out I would be leaving in a different car. I was certain this was all a "trick" and that somehow, I would be with my brothers soon. The wait for the second car dragged on from minutes to several hours.

I was never given a chance to ask questions about the separation of me and my brothers. I was told simply that I needed to be ready for my car.

I felt that I had been tricked. How could anyone be so cruel? First, there was the separation from my mother, now the tragic separation from my younger brothers.

# Chapter 3
## Don't Cry Over Spilled Milk

Several hours slipped by as I sat on the porch still waiting for my ride. The thought that I may never see my brothers again started to feel real. How did this just happen? Somehow, I knew I needed to think about something else. I managed to tell myself none of this was my fault.

It didn't take long before my thoughts took over and I began to wrestle with ideas and even ways to trick these people into taking me back to see my brothers. The only story that I came up with was to lie about having a serious medical problem that gave me only 6 months to live.

My daydreaming continued as I struggled to come up with more creative stories that would get me back with my brothers until I was startled by one of the neighborhood dogs who lunged on top of my paper bag. The next thing I remember, the dog was running into the streets with my favorite and only sweater. Without hesitation, I leaped off the front porch swing, grabbed my paper bag and ran after the dog to rescue my sweater which was special and carried memories about my mother.

My mother had given up a trip to the beauty salon to allow me to buy this blue polka dot sweater. The more I remembered the story behind the sweater, the faster I ran after the dog. The race finally came to an end when the dog became distracted by another dog who was feasting on some type of roadkill.

I quickly stuffed the grimy sweater into my paper bag and hurried back to the Emergency Group Home. On my way back, it occurred to me that a lot of time had passed. This thought lead to the possibility that the Emergency home may have called the police to make a missing person's report. Quickly, the thought of being seen as a "runaway" popped into my head and I panicked. With this thought, I remember running back to the Emergency Home as fast as I could. Gasping for breath, I made it back only to find an empty porch with no one in sight.

After catching my breath and seeing that I wasn't in trouble, hunger pains kicked in.

A part of me wanted to dash into the house and say, "what's for lunch?" However, the stubborn side would not allow me to go anywhere near the kitchen. I sat on the porch thinking about hunger and how it gave me control. It helped me feel stronger rather than weak. This control didn't last very long, as my hunger pains won over and I was ready to ask for something to eat.

Growing up, I was never one to ask for help. I felt this to be a sign of weakness. Being poor and having a parent who depended on me reinforced the importance of patience and putting others first. Unfortunately, today would not be a day for me to show patience or put others before me.

Slowly, I made my way towards the front door and peeped through the torn screen before finding enough courage to enter the house. The aroma of the food drifted out the door inviting, or daring, me to come into the house. Finally, I told myself, "Enough is enough, just get it over with and go on in."

Cautiously, I opened the door and tip-toed down the hallway. As I approached the kitchen, I heard several voices, the clanging of dishes and a female voice say, "Does anyone know if the overnight girl has been picked up yet?"

All of a sudden, my hunger pains disappeared and so did I. The mere thought of food made me sick to my stomach. I quickly and quietly turned around and returned to the front porch to wait for my ride. After dozing off for a short period of time, I was wakened by a distant humming sound. I hoped that the distant sound was coming from an automobile. Not just any automobile, but one that would be taking me away from this place.

A small two-door yellow car pulled into the driveway and out stepped a petite lady dressed in fancy church-like clothes topped off with a large floppy hat that was two sizes too big for her head. As I was unsure who this lady was, I continued swinging and minding my own business until I heard my name, "You must be Lauren. I was told I would find a cute little girl waiting for me. I'm Mrs. Gertrude."

"Yes ma'am, I am Lauren. It's nice that you're finally here. I mean, I'm ready to go. Do you know where my brothers are?"

"I do, why don't we talk about that in the car? Wait just a minute or two while I go and find someone who works here to tell them that you're leaving." I almost wanted to tell this lady everything about this place. She left to go inside. But like she said, I could wait and talk about things once we were in the car. The next thing I remember, Mrs. Gertrude was back and asked if I needed help with my brown paper bag.

"No Ma'am. It's not very heavy. I'm used to carrying it around."

Once we were settled in the car, Mrs. Gertrude began to talk to me as if she had known me forever. She even offered me a "squirrel nut." I remember thinking, "Wow; she even likes one of my favorite pieces of candy so she can't be all that bad."

Our conversation continued, and we both shared our likes and dislikes surrounding foods, TV shows and our favorite holidays. After about fifteen minutes of talking, it occurred to me that Mrs. Gertrude had not given me any information about my brothers. Things were going so well between the two of us, I didn't want to spoil it, but I had to know about my brothers. I literally had to count to ten before I blurted it out.

"Mrs. Gertrude, would you please tell me about my brothers? I have to know."

"Well of course dear, I will tell you what I know. Your brothers have been taken to a very nice home. They are living together and will grow up having the same mom and dad."

"Mrs. Gertrude, will I be able to visit my brothers and spend time with them?"

"That is a question I can't answer. But I will find out for you. I know you love your brothers very much and can see how see how important they are too you."

By now, I knew that Mrs. Gertrude had done the best she could. But it still wasn't enough. Quiet filled the car, as our conversations came to a gentle halt. In some odd way, I felt it was only respectable to let Mrs. Gertrude know I was feeling rather tired and would like to rest for the remainder of the trip. My true intentions involved secretively crying myself to sleep until arriving at the new home. Not only did I fall asleep for the rest of the ride, but I also had an incredible dream that my brothers were standing in the yard of my new home with balloons that said, "Welcome to our new home, sister."

It didn't turn out that way. Rather, once again, I was greeted by more strangers. "Lauren, we are here. Can you start waking up? I have a small snack for you. While you were sleeping, I stopped and bought you apple juice and peanut butter crackers. Would you like to eat them before going into the house?"

"No Ma'am. Can I take them with me to have later?"

"Sure, you can. Well let's get going, honey, it's getting late."

With some reluctance, I gathered my brown paper bag and followed Mrs. Gertrude up to the white sterile-looking house that was surrounded by a four-foot chain link fence. The front yard was missing any toys, trash, or evidence that any children lived in this home.

Mrs. Gertrude gently took hold of my small clammy hand and stepped up to the door. Immediately, the door opened, and we were greeted by a Mr. Jones, who was introduced as the manager of what turned out to be a group home.

Mr. Jones was a husky man who had an out-of-control grayish beard covering half his face. He appeared caught off guard by our arrival. He informed us that Mrs. Jones had unexpectedly received a call to go visit a sick friend at the hospital. Mr. Jones, however, reassured both me and Mrs. Gertrude that she would take over upon her return. Surprisingly, Mrs. Gertrude turned to me and said, "Well Lauren, it looks like you're in good hands."

I immediately began to feel a little angry and scared, seeing that the one lady I trusted was leaving me. While holding in my anger and refusing direct eye contact, I said, "Mrs. Gertrude, I am OK, See you later." After saying our goodbyes, Mr. Jones showed me my bedroom. He asked if Mrs. Gertrude would be coming back later to bring my personal belongings. I replied, "No Sir," I have them here in my bag."

Mr. Jones replied with a puzzled look, "Are you sure these are the only clothes you have?"

"Yes Sir." Mr. Jones quickly shifted to another subject and asked if I was hungry. Before I could answer his question, he informed me that dinner would be ready in an hour. He also told me that Mrs. Jones would return home shortly to join us for dinner.

I spent the next 30 to 45 minutes in my room organizing my clothes in a gray plastic storage bin that had a piece of tape attached with my name on it. My bedroom was about the size of a large walk-in closet. I had a twin-size bed that was covered with a dull gray colored fleece blanket. There was no headboard and oddly no pillows. The walls were bare. In fact, there was no evidence that a picture had ever been hung or a mark put on the walls. The walls reminded me of hospital walls.

As I finished un-packing my clothes, I found a book, *Charlotte's Web*, and my favorite doll at the bottom of my brown paper bag. I decided that I would use these two items to make my room look pretty and cheery. Having only a few seconds to stare at my now newly decorated bedroom, a loud knock came to my door.

"Lauren, Mrs. Jones just pulled into the driveway. Go wash up and come out for dinner."

I wasn't sure where to sit at the table and continued standing until Mrs. Jones entered the room and formally greeted me. Mrs. Jones was the complete opposite of Mr. Jones. She was a tall, olive skin woman who appeared to be somewhat older than Mr. Jones. Dinner was finally served, and I learned that night that seating arrangements were in fact important. I was informed that at the next meal, breakfast, I would have a piece of tape with my name on it representing my chair assignment. Throughout the course of dinner, Mr. and Mrs. Jones initially talked among themselves before actually focusing on my stay at their home. The conversation and dialogue between the three of us was more casual. I was questioned about some of my likes and dislikes, hobbies, etc.

About half-way through the meal, Mrs. Jones noticed that I had not been drinking my milk. She quickly encouraged me to "Drink up your milk, it's getting late."

I remember responding, "Mrs. Jones, I would rather have a glass of water because milk makes me throw up."

Mrs. Jones quickly informed me that I had to make an attempt to drink the milk before getting a glass of water. All I could think of at that moment was there was going to be trouble. I tried my best to drink the glass of milk, but the truth be known, the last time I had milk was in infancy. According to my mother, I stopped drinking milk when I was an infant and the doctor concluded I had some type of medical complication.

The pivotal point of that evening came when I tried to drink the milk for the last time, and I threw up all over the dining table. Mrs. Jones was furious. I thought she only had herself to blame. I tried to explain and warn her about my problems with drinking milk, but she just didn't want to listen.

I remember Mrs. Jones shouting, "Get up from this table and go to your room. You aren't even allowed to finish your dinner. I'm sending you to bed early."

Once I left the table, I thought to myself, "I'll never go back to that stupid table ever again. I will starve before going back." Feeling many things that night...tired, angry, abandoned, and stupid, I desperately needed something to help me feel better.

After tossing and turning, I still couldn't come up with anything to help get me through the night. Just as I was about to drift off to sleep, I remembered an old saying that my grandmother would often use when she'd go through a tough time but somehow make the best of it. That saying was "Don't cry over spilled milk." In some strange way, remembering that saying not only helped me get to sleep that night, but it also continued to help me for the rest of my life.

# Chapter 4
# Moving On

There was nothing exciting or magical about my last five days at the group home. I stayed mostly to myself, camped out in my assigned bedroom, and came out only when meals were served. The true highlight during these final days was the tall, plastic glasses of water at each meal in place of milk.

Thinking back, it was the water that kept me on my "P's and Q's" as my grandmother would have said. The idea of running away really never left my mind. Somehow, I was able to beat the devil at his game and avoid this temptation. I knew running away was not the right thing to do.

The last 24 hours at this home were the hardest. However, I knew it was only a matter of time before I would be away from this awful place. Having patience and remaining calm until then would not be easy.

I also knew I had to suck it up and be that strong girl that I knew I could be. It finally came to me that I would be better off spending time alone in the bedroom away from others. The last thing I needed to do would be to mouth off to these workers; who knows what would happen to me.

I settled for spending the majority of those 24 hours alone, locked inside my bedroom. During my alone time, I was able to think about both the good and bad moments I had experienced since coming to this home.

The most horrifying moment that I'll never forget was being punished for refusing milk at dinner. There really weren't many good moments. I knew I was not placed here to make any memories or friends and guess what, I didn't. It was all business.

With very little notice, my stomach reminded me that I needed to eat something soon and to not oversleep or miss dinner. I decided that I would set the alarm clock, as I still had two hours to rest before dinner would be served.

The next thing I remember, I found myself reaching for the alarm clock while at the same time, knocking it off the bedside table and under the bed. The annoying sound still failed to give me any motivation to silence the sound. This decision resulted in more shut eye.

Three hours later, I was startled and abruptly awakened by an unfriendly voice yelling out, "Are you sleeping in there?" Before I could even respond, I heard. "I'm coming in there now."

As I tried to get out of bed, I heard the lock on my door turning and a small woman shuffled across the floor carrying a spiral notebook with an unsharpened pencil.

Since I had never met this woman, I had no idea what her intentions were. For a quick moment, I had lots of thoughts racing through my head. Some were good and some bad. There was an awkward period of silence, as this mystery worker fumbled through her spiral notebook. I became more and more uncomfortable with this silence and started to ask a question only to be interrupted by the woman.

"You have slept right on through the dinner hour. The kitchen is closed. There will be no more food served until morning. Breakfast will be at 7:00 a.m."

Before I could even get a word in, the woman continued to mumble on.

"I know that you are leaving here tomorrow to go live somewhere else. Now, let's get started with looking at your clothes. I need for you to put all of your clothes on the bed for me to look at."

For a moment, I felt like mouthing off at this old lady. As a child, I was always taught to respect one's elders but at that moment, respect was not on my mind.

"Do you think that I stole something from this house?"

"Honey, I don't know. But it's my job to make sure you didn't. Now go on. Hurry along and show me what's in those dresser drawers."

"You really want me to show you what I got? O.k., I'll show you."

"Yes, I do. Now stop fiddling around and get it."

The next thing that I remember is that I leaped out of my bed and began grabbing the few items that I owned and threw them onto the bed.

"Now, slow down missy. You are getting a little out of control here," she barked at me.

"Okay. Miss Lady, do your job. But I am not a stealer. My mother taught me right from wrong. She also took me to church every Sunday."

"I'm finished honey. Of course, you are not a thief. But I'm just doing my job. Good night."

The rest of the night was exhausting. I felt ashamed, guilty, and angry for yelling at the old woman. I also felt personally attacked and treated unfairly for being accused of being a thief and a liar. However, the best part of the night was falling asleep knowing that it would be my last night living at this place. Sweet dreams.

The day finally arrived for me to leave this place. Everything was in order and ready to go. I woke up early and had a decent breakfast. My brown paper bag had been checked and had passed inspection. The social worker was scheduled to pick me up within the hour. I decided to wait inside the house until she arrived. During my wait, I was approached by another house worker who demanded that I open my brown paper bag to allow her to search my belongings. I initially refused, informing her that my bags had been already searched. I was told by this person that she would be checking my bag every 30 minutes until my departure. At first, I wanted to grab my brown paper bag and run. How much more could I take? These thoughts were interrupted by the sound of the doorbell. It was the social worker, two hours late! I recall feeling ever so grateful, yet at the same time, I was furious for her tardiness.

"Mrs. Jones, I've been waiting all morning for you. What happened? This home has been like a bad dream. The lady that worked today searched my bag every 30 minutes thinking I would have the nerve to steal from this dungeon. I told her that I was not a thief and that she needed to back off. This place is not safe. Mrs. Jones, you should talk to these people."

"Honey, try and calm down, everything will be O.k. Of course, you are not a thief. Maybe the lady was just doing her job. Could I take a look in your bag?"

"No, No. No, you are just like them. I thought you were different. So now I can't trust you either. Oh, are you just doing your job too?" *Don't even bother to answer my question because it doesn't matter. The damage has been done. There is no going back to trusting anyone.* "I don't have anything else to say to you."

After a few seconds passed, with no more information from Mrs. Jones, it hit me that I had no idea where she was taking me. Maybe, I should start up a conversation. I needed to be careful because I needed her to know that I was still mad at her for wanting to check my bag.

Finally, we were on our way. I felt lost and did not know what to say or think. "Mrs. Jones, I may need to use the bathroom soon. Are we almost there?"

"Honey, I know you're still upset but I do need to talk to you about where I'm taking you. But first, we will stop to have a bathroom break."

"No, I can wait. I mean if it's not too long You can go ahead and tell me where you're taking me."

"Honey, I am taking you to the foster home where your brother, Richard, lives."

"Are you serious? Why didn't you tell me this before?"

"Well, I wanted to tell you earlier, but you were so angry with me, I wasn't sure you would believe me."

"To be honest with you, it is hard to trust you. But I don't think you would play a trick on me about this. Would you?"

"Of course not. So, we should be at Richard's foster home in about 45 minutes. Should we plan on stopping for a snack and bathroom break before then?"

"Yes ma'am, that would be good. Mrs. Jones, thank you."

"You are so welcome. I'm so happy to be able to do something nice for you."

As much as I wanted to believe and trust Mrs. Jones, it was still touch and go. I would just have to wait this out before I could get excited. As my grandmother would say, I would not count any chickens until I see them hatch.

# Chapter 5
# Reunited with Richard

My excitement was difficult to hide as I hummed along to tunes from the radio and occasionally snapped my fingers when I thought the social worker wasn't looking my way. Despite that day being the happiest I'd been in months; I knew that getting my hopes up would probably just backfire and I'd be let down again. So, the only thing I knew to do was to protect myself and that meant putting up a wall.

"My, you sure are in a good mood today," the social worker commented.

"Not really, I'm just enjoying the music, like any other day."

"So, are you ready for this big day?"

"Yes, of course I am. Wouldn't you want to see your brother after someone tricked you and took him away? Don't you know that was a dirty thing to do? What would you do if such a thing happened to you?"

"Well honey we should be there in about ten minutes. Now get yourself together."

What could she possibly mean, "Get myself together?" It became clear to me that this woman was not interested in me or how I felt. I decided that I would not waste any more of my time on this social worker. Instead, I thought about coming up with the perfect words to say when I was face-to-face to Richard.

I must have thought of 20 different ways of how I could tell Richard how much I had missed him. However, they all sounded "corny." Darn it, surely, he would just be glad to see me and would not be thinking of hearing any "perfect words." As a child, my grandmother's favorite motto was, "actions speak louder than words." So, I had made my decision, I would forget about coming up with perfect words and give Richard the biggest hug he'd probably had in a long time.

After I had made my decision about Richard, I told myself that I had nothing to worry about. The conversation that I had with myself not only took away any worry or doubt, but it also put me right to sleep. I suppose it was more like I had a "cat nap" because it didn't last very long. I heard someone barking orders that I needed to get my things ready and collect any trash that I may have dropped.

It only took a few minutes until I realized that I would soon be face-to face with my brother, Richard. Suddenly, my mind started racing again with lots of thoughts and worries about Richard and I being together again.

The first thought that popped into my mind was could this be a set-up or a trick? It was so hard for me to believe or trust in people since I was taken away from my mother.

I was lied to by the welfare people when I was told that my mother would get well soon and we would then go back home. I knew that would never happen. I found out my mother went to a hospital for "crazy" people and would probably never be the same.

Once I knew that going back home to live with my mother would never happen, I started thinking about other family members jumping in and racing to take us in. When that didn't happen, I had settled on the possibility of my dad. I even wondered, "Why couldn't our dad take care of us?" Well, that didn't happen either. There was never a whole lot said about my dad, other than "he was a drunk" and would never be able to get us kids back. There had been lots of rumors that some relatives were ashamed and embarrassed by my family's problems and in the end turned their back on four innocent, helpless children. After I found out that my own "blood relatives" wanted nothing to do us, I wanted to somehow tell them how much I hated them for being so selfish and mean.

I could feel myself getting angry all over again and I knew that I wanted to be happy when I saw Richard. I knew that we should be getting close to Richard's house.

"We are two blocks away," the social worker commented. "Do you suppose your brother will be waiting out in the front yard for you?"

"Hum, I guess the sooner we get there the sooner we will know." I knew my answer was not what the social worker wanted to hear. She pretty much ignored me until we arrived at Richard's house.

With little warning, the social worker blurted out, "Well, we made it, and I don't see anyone. Let's just go to the door and show ourselves."

Before I could get out of the car, the social worker had already made her way to the front door. I decided to stay put until I saw the front door open. The social worker must have knocked on the door a dozen times with no one hearing her, or could it be that no one was home?

I knew that this social worker would not stay on the porch and knock forever. She had other "fish to fry" as my grandmother would say. I had expected the worker to give up on Richard and his foster family and call it a day. I had already made up my mind that I was not leaving this yard and would not be going back with her. As the social worker walked off the porch, I was ready to bolt out of the car and never look back. I cautiously sat back in the car seat waiting for the social worker to get settled into the front seat and then I would make my move. She never made it back to the car, as she instead started walking towards the backyard of Richard's home.

*Maybe I spoke too soon.* Was it possible that this social worker wasn't giving up after all? I continued to stay focused on where she was going and what she had planned to do. It wasn't very long until I figured out what the worker was about to do. She somehow saw a side-back door, one last chance to find if Richard was home.

*How did I miss seeing this back door?* My grandmother had always told me that I had eyes in the back of my head. I never understood the real meaning of this until today. Now, this social worker had eyes in the back of her head. She knocked only once, and it was at that time a parade of people started walking out the door. However, Richard was not included in this parade.

*Where was Richard?* He should have been the first or second person to race out from the door. I managed to keep my eyes glued to the back door. I still had hopes that Richard would make his way out and rush past all these strange people. The longer it took for Richard to show himself, the more I thought something had gone wrong.

Then out of the blue, I heard a loud shout and turned to find Richard staring at me through the car window. I wasn't sure which direction he came from. I never saw him walk out the back door. In the end, none of that mattered. All that mattered was I was finally face-to-face with my beloved brother.

"Sister, sister, you are here. You didn't forget to come? Come on, get out of the car and let's go inside my new home." It was a relief that Richard wanted to see me and didn't hate me after all.

"Okay, just a minute, I have a gift for you, but I need to find it. I panicked for a moment, as I could not find the special gift that I had wanted Richard to have.

"A gift? You bought me a gift? It ain't even my birthday."

"I know it's not your birthday. But today is a special day and we will celebrate!"

"Okay, what is it?"

I somehow managed to find and save the book *Jack and the Beanstalk*, one of Richard's favorite childhood books, to give him. Before he managed to open the bag, I gently asked if he could wait to open the gift until we were inside. I saw the disappointment on his face but was quick to reach out and give him a big hug which seemed to be the next best thing to his gift.

"Richard let's go inside first so that I can meet everyone. Then, you can open up your gift."

Sister, I'm so glad that you finally got here. I have been sad without you.

Where are our brothers?"

"We can talk about all that later. Today is our special day and we are going to celebrate."

Much of that day was spent getting to know my new foster parents, the rules of the house and hanging out with my brother. Mary and Jerry Sims were the foster parents who had been taking care of Richard. They had a son, Jason, who was the same age as Richard, along with a two-year-old daughter, Denise.

Mr. and Mrs. Sims were young; they seemed to be about the age of my mom. Mary Sims was a "looker" with straight blond hair, sparkling blue eyes and a curvy body that I learned got her a lot of attention, especially from Jerry.

Jerry was tall, thin, and had unusually long fingernails for a man. I often wondered why a man would want such long nails. He seemed proud of his long fingernails, as he later bragged about opening a can of sardines with his fingernails. Perhaps this explained why he never wanted to cut them. I thought they looked wicked and not suited for a man.

Jerry also played baseball with his friends from work and often invited Mary and the kids to his games. The funny thing is, Mary never went to see Jerry play and never let us go either. I never understood why a wife would not go and watch her husband play a game that he liked and be proud of him.

As time went on, it became clear why Mary and Jerry didn't do a lot of things together. Mary did not keep any secrets about Jerry's drinking. She would tell anyone about it. She sometimes yelled and screamed at Jerry when he came home smelling like alcohol. In some ways, they reminded me of my own mom and dad. There were times when Jerry's drinking got a little out of hand. He would make fun of Mary and say things about her that were mean.

Mary never said anything to us about Jerry's drinking. She mainly talked to her mother about Jerry and sometimes she would call her mother crying. It wasn't a secret that Jerry and Mary's mother did not like each other. To be honest, I never liked Mary's mother either. She treated her own grandchildren, Jason, and Denise, like a prince and princess while she often reminded me and Richard that we were different.

Mary's mother eventually moved in with us and that's when the real trouble began. I happened to overhear an argument between Mary and Jerry that she never asked him about her mother moving in. Things became touch and go for a while, as Jerry sometimes would not come home after work.

I always tried to pay attention to Mary and Jerry's troubles because I never wanted Richard to hear or know anything about it. It was my goal to protect Richard as much as I could. My brother had been through enough and clearly didn't need to worry or fear that something bad might happen to us.

Richard and I seemed to reconnect quickly and became closer to each other. I played the role of big sister and sometimes stepped up to being his caretaker. This was necessary for me to do because he was often treated differently from Jason and certainly was not favored by Mary's mother, the "wicked grandmother." The extreme favoritism that was given to Mary's kids was certainly not right, but there was nothing I could do about it.

On several occasions, I found Jason and his grandmother picking on Richard. It seemed like Jason was following in his own grandmother's shoes taunting and bullying Richard. I was always on guard with Jason and his grandmother. I knew they were two peas in a pod.

But the struggle with the "wicked grandmother" was not the only complicated part of living at the Sims house. On one occasion, I overhead a telephone conversation that told me trouble was coming. This phone conversation began with a whimpering female voice that quickly changed to a sob. I quickly recognized the voice being Mary's. It was only a few seconds later that I knew Mary was having this phone conversation with her mother. I felt trapped in not being able to leave my room; while at the same time, I wanted to hear the conversation. Mary continued the conversation sobbing and then finally blurted out, "I followed Jerry… and saw him out with a young woman. It's over. I can't… live with him anymore. I can't trust the man. He doesn't love me anymore. The children…will have to understand. They will… have to adjust."

My heart sank and my knees trembled. I had to get out of the house as fast as my legs would take me. I managed to escape without being seen. Once I was outside, I spotted my bike and decided that a ride around the block was exactly what I needed. There were so many thoughts flashing through my mind. "Would this end up being another move to a different home? How could this be happening again? This could not happen to me and Richard. We belong together.

# Chapter 6
## Opportunity Knocks

I continued to hide the secret of knowing about Mary and Jerry's marital problems. However, it was only two weeks after that shocking conversation that Jerry packed his bags and moved out. I later found out that Jerry left Mary for a younger, prettier woman he had met at work. In some ways, Jerry reminded me of my own dad. They both left their wives for younger women and neither of them ever seemed bothered by their decision.

Mary never breathed a word about why Jerry left her. However, it wasn't a secret that her mother couldn't been happier to have Jerry gone. It had only been a matter of 24 hours before Mary's mother stepped into the role as "Big Mama." Her new role kept me on my toes, as I had to watch her like a hawk to make sure she wasn't mistreating Richard.

It was no secret that Big Mama played favorites when it came to Jason and Denise, as she made sure they got first dibs on everything. On a few occasions, I tried to spy on Big Mama to see what really happened when she was left alone at home with us kids. The one time I caught her in the act, she was secretively handing Jason candy and gave him a "Shhhhhh" before she started to exit her bedroom.

While I knew I had very little control over Big Mama, it never stopped me from being on guard when it came to protecting Richard. It seemed that life for all of us moved on, as Jerry became more like a sad memory from our past. It was only a few months after Jerry left when Mary started to date other men and seemed to be happy.

It was about that same time that I started to make friends and had things to look forward to. One of those things included boys. I never thought of myself as being pretty. While I never thought about my looks, it suddenly became important, as I knew that pretty girls ended up getting attention from boys. Boys also chose the prettier girls over the ugly ones. So, when I officially got my first, true boyfriend Johnny, I had a hard time believing that a guy would want to have me as his girlfriend. Johnny was known as the most popular guy in the neighborhood and girls would camp outside waiting for his school bus to drop him off to catch a glimpse of him.

I never knew what he saw in me. He could have had any girl that he wanted. But why he chose me was a mystery. Johnny wasn't like all the other boys; he knew how to treat a girl. What I liked about him was he didn't feel sorry for me and never thought of me as a "foster child." Mary never knew that Johnny was my boyfriend. He had been a secret for a long time. The truth was, I was afraid that Mary would not approve, and I would lose Johnny as a boyfriend.

The first real alone time with Johnny was at the school's fall carnival. On that particular night, we skipped bobbing for apples, the cake walk, and picking up ducks. Instead, we spent our time in the dance hall. We danced and danced and then we kissed. It was not a pucker up kiss, it was a real "French Kiss." It was a magical night that I didn't want to end. I knew that this night would stay with me forever.

I knew Mary would be picking me up promptly after the carnival, so I said my goodbye to Johnny a little early that night and waited out front for her. I must have caught a break, as Mary was not alone when she picked me up. She had been out with a girlfriend and was distracted by conversation with her. I decided not to interrupt their talking and hoped that Mary would forget that I was in the car. The last thing I wanted was to be asked a million questions about the carnival.

Once we arrived home, I attempted to make a quick get-away after thanking Mary for taking me to the carnival. But this was interrupted as Mary blurted out. "So, did you have a good time tonight?"

"Yes, ma'am I had a great time. I'm kinda tired so I think I'll go to bed now." Thinking that I was finished with our conversation, I turned to walk down the hall to my bedroom but was once again caught off guard by Mary.

"Lauren, I forgot to tell you that your social worker called today and left a message that she was coming to visit you and Richard tomorrow."

"What? Tomorrow? That's crazy, tomorrow is Saturday. Darn, does that women work on the weekend?"

"Well, I guess she does. Now go on to bed. She will be here around noon."

"Does Richard know about that this visit?"

"No, I forgot to tell him."

"Good, don't bother to tell him. He doesn't need to know or worry about anything."

"O.K, Goodnight."

"Well, you don't have to worry about Richard, because the social worker, Mrs. Jones, wants to talk to you alone without Richard."

"Why? Does she have some bad news for me?"

"No, it's actually good news. She wants to talk to you about a family who is interested in adopting you."

"What about Richard? Does this family want Richard?"

"I don't think so. The family has asked to adopt a girl."

"That's crazy. I'm not leaving here without my brother. If they don't want Richard, then they don't get me."

"Now, now, I want you to just listen and talk to Mrs. Jones when she arrives here tomorrow."

"I suppose if she drives all the way out here, I could listen to her story."

It was hard to sleep that night, as I tossed and turned until the next morning. I had multiple confusing dreams throughout the night about doors being opened and closed around me. As I found my dreams too disturbing to fall back to sleep, I decided to write a five-page love letter to my sweet dear Johnny. When the letter was completed, and I was still wide awake, I realized my chances of getting any sleep would be slim. I looked over at the clock and it read 6:55 a.m. I decided to take an early bath and then quietly watch some of my favorite cartoons.

Mary was next to rise; pots and pans rattled around in the kitchen followed by the aroma of bacon and eggs. The smell of the early morning food lured me out of my room in hopes I could squeeze a little more information out of Mary regarding today's visit with Mrs. Jones.

"Good morning. How did you sleep?" Mary asked.

"Not so well. I guess I'm a little worried about today's visit. Have I done something wrong around here?"

"Of course not. Are you hungry for some bacon and eggs?"

"I guess so."

I found it odd that Mary changed the subject so quickly; she is normally overly eager to offer her opinion on most matters. I decided rather than challenge Mary, I would continue to go along with the program. I ate my breakfast alone, as Mary was preoccupied preparing for Mrs. Jones arrival. Just as I was loading my dirty dishes in sink, both Richard and Jason made their way into the kitchen stumbling around each other looking for their favorite box of cereal.

"Good morning. It's about time y'all got up. It's too bad that all the cartoons are over."

Richard quickly looked my way and grinned.

Jason, on the other hand, blurted out "that's a lie."

"O.k., calm down, I was only joking. There is still plenty of time for you watch cartoons."

Both Richard and Jason dashed into the den with their bowls of frosted flakes to watch Jason's favorite cartoon shows. As I continued cleaning the kitchen table, I looked up at the clock and realized that Mrs. Jones was due to arrive in 15 minutes.

I immediately felt the need to find Mary to inform her of the time. For a moment, I panicked, because Mary was nowhere to be found. Just as I began to call out Mary's name, she exited from her mother's room. Before I could utter a word, she informed me to prepare for Mrs. Jones's arrival. There was clearly something different about Mary that left me feeling a little nervous.

There was very little time that morning to confront her about what was really going on. After giving this more thought, I went to find Mary to ask her more questions, but I never got a chance, as the doorbell rang signaling Mrs. Jones's arrival. Mary greeted the social worker and without hesitation called out for me to join her for a private chat in the dining room. It had been at least 6 months since my last face-to-face contact with Mrs. Jones. Mary proceeded to make formal introductions and shared the progress I had made over the past months. Shortly after all the formalities, Mary politely excused herself and assured Mrs. Jones that our conservation would be away from others. I thought to myself, "away from others?" This must be serious.

Mrs. Jones began our conversation by asking typical questions of how I had been doing and what my experience had been like living at the Sims. I had wondered if she knew about Jerry's leaving. I knew that I wasn't going to utter a word about their situation.

"It's so great to hear how well you've fit in here at the Sims."

"Yeah, I have loved being here with Richard. I wouldn't trade it for anything."

"Well, that's what I'm here to talk about today."

"What do you mean?"

"There is a family who is interested in adopting you. Their son died in a car accident two years ago and they are finally ready to get another child."

"Oh, really?" I spoke.

"Yes, and they think you just might be the lucky one."

"What about Richard? Are they interested in him?"

"They are not interested in Richard."

"Well, that's crazy. How could they want me without him?"

"Honey, sometimes it just works out that way. Now they want you to come and spend a weekend with them. They are excited about getting to know you. These people are not just ordinary people. They are able to provide for you. They can give you things that you have never had."

"Like what?"

"Well, like piano lessons, private school, new clothes, vacations, beautiful home, a college education and so much more."

"Well, I'm still not sure about this. I mean my brother is still worth so much more than those things."

"I will make a deal with you. Why don't you just go for a weekend visit and see how things go before you make a final decision."

"If I go for the weekend, will I be able to come back here to stay with Richard?"

"That will be our plan."

"So run along and pack enough clothes for the weekend so we can get going."

"You mean I am leaving today to go for a weekend visit?"

"Yes. They are waiting for you."

In some God-awful way, a surge of excitement bolted through my body as I thought of piano lessons, new clothes, college, and a beautiful home as I dashed into my room to pack a few clothes into my brown paper bag. The next thing I ventured to do was to find Richard to say goodbye until Monday. Richard was nowhere to be found. Mary quickly informed me that Jason and Richard had received an opportunity to attend a matinee movie with a neighbor next door and wouldn't be home for several hours.

Mary assured me that Richard would be fine until I returned home on Monday. While I had mixed emotions about leaving that day, I honestly felt in my heart that I would see Richard again. So, with that thought in mind, I grabbed my paper bag and out the door I went.

# Chapter 7
# The Audition

The excitement of getting a new home gave me hope yet it also left me with butterflies in my stomach that I didn't quite understand. I had so many questions that kept popping up that I needed answered. These questions came to me like bolts of lightning. The distraction of thinking about getting a new home faded quickly, as I started to wonder if I made a mistake by agreeing to leave the Sims. I was never one to agree or easily give in when I felt pressured or taken advantage of. Rather, I was always known for my "stubbornness" and for asking 100 questions before I could make a decision. This would be one time that I must have been caught off guard and talked into making a quick decision.

I thought maybe I should ask the social worker to turn the car around because I had every right to get those questions answered before making a final decision. The more that I tried to convince myself to do this, a little voice inside my head whispered, "it's too late to turn back now."

While I blamed myself for jumping the gun on my decision to leave the Sims home, I tried to remind myself, I could always return back to the Sims home. It was still confusing to me as how a family could invite or be interested in a child they've never seen before? Wouldn't this be a risk and a possible disappointment for a family? Suppose a family is disappointed that a child isn't pretty or even smart enough? What would happen then? Would that family get rid of a child or simply send them back?

I found myself peering into the driver's overhead mirror to catch a glimpse of what my face looked like. I was never told I was a pretty girl. The only time I ever felt cute or pretty was when I would catch my first boyfriend, Johnny winking at me. You would have thought these winks were as good as kisses. I felt like a queen every time he fluttered one my way. I never learned how to wink. I probably practiced for 6 months but just could not get the hang of it.

I never felt special growing up. However, I became responsible and, in many ways, that got me a lot of attention. I knew my being responsible would have pleased my grandmother. However, as a girl, being pretty or even feeling pretty was still important. After I realized the social worker would not be going back to the Sims or answering any of my questions, I decided to just sit back and "let nature take its course," one of my grandmother's sayings.

I continued thinking more about this family and the possible reasons behind their interest in me. Only time will tell. "Life is a gamble," another one of my grandmother's favorite sayings.

The social worker had very little to say during the first part of the drive but without any notice that changed. "Aren't you excited about this weekend? It's possible that Mr. and Mrs. Dew might just make up their mind that they want you to live with them for good." Pausing only briefly, she continued, "It's not every day that a child gets this lucky you know. Now, you are a smart girl, so show them just how smart you really are."

"And what if none of this happens with the Dews?" I blurted out. "What's next?"

"Well, honey, we will just have to wait and see. But just remember, you know how to act and have all the right words that will sell yourself."

"Are you saying that I am for sale? Now that is just crazy. That sounds like some work of the devil. I don't want anybody to try to buy me. We can just call this whole trip off right now and you can turn your car around and take me back to my brother."

After not getting a response from her, I continued, "Besides, what if I blurt out the wrong words?" It sounds more and more like I'm trying out for a school play. The big difference here is there are no rehearsals; it's showtime.

"Now, now honey, is that supposed to be a joke?"

"No ma'am, it's not a joke. It's the truth."

There was not a lot of talking between the social worker and me for the next twenty minutes or so. I continued to wonder why a rich family would waste their weekend on a poor girl who had very little to give. The only thought that entered my mind was this family had been told about my "great housekeeping skills." That's it, they want me because I can clean their big house for them. Why didn't I think of that earlier? Well at least, I'd be valued for something.

After quickly sneaking a peak at the social worker and finding her deep in thought, I decided to nod off and rest my brain. I couldn't have slept more than fifteen minutes before I was awakened to loud hiccupping sounds.

Before I knew what I was doing, I found myself gazing over at her.

"Honey, what's wrong?"

"What do you mean?"

"You're looking at me."

"Oh, I was just thinking about the dream I had."

"Oh, do you want to tell me about it?"

"It's not really that important. It would probably be boring to you."

She responded to me with a tone that I wasn't sure was genuine. "Of course, what you have to say is important and certainly not boring. So, please share it with me."

Well, I guess I could tell you about some of it."

"Great, then after we finish with your dream, I need to discuss something very important with you about Mr. and Mrs. Dew before we arrive at their home. So, lets' get started."

"Well, maybe you should go first then. It sounds like you have some pretty serious news."

"No, no, I want you to go first."

"O.K., in my dream, when Mr. and Mrs. Dew met me, they liked me a lot and even thought I was kinda cute. The next best part of the dream was they had a house cleaner, and I didn't become the house maid. Now, for the best part of the dream. The Dews made a decision to keep me."

I had expected some kind of reaction or comment from the social worker, rather, she decided to go right into her agenda about what she needed to share. "O.K. honey, now there's something important we need to talk about."

I began to feel a little nervous, as a quiet voice deep within me cautiously echoed "danger ahead" and "prepare yourself for cover and protection."

"Well sweetheart, Mr. and Mrs. Dew lost a very special person in their family two years ago. They were sad for a very long time after they lost this person. But now they are better, and they want to have another special person in their family."

"Who was this person that they lost?"

"They lost their son. They bought their 16 yr.-old son his first car and he wrecked it and died."

The first words that came out of my mouth were, "Turn this car around and take me back. I can't go to this home. I will never fit in."

"Honey, calm down, this family needs and wants another child. They are ready and willing to look you over and give you a chance. We can't let them down. They are expecting us to arrive in exactly fifteen minutes."

"Are you really making me go?"

"Yes. Now, we are almost there. Remember this could become your new home."

I was at a loss for words and felt powerless. Was it possible that this could be my new home? Was this family ready to move on and get a new child? A replacement?

"Honey, we're almost here, just a few a few blocks away. Take a look at these fancy houses. Just think, you may be living in one of these big houses soon."

"Wow, these are big houses. They look more like castles than regular houses. I wonder how long it would take to clean a house that size?"

"Honey, you can worry about that later. You need to meet the family first."

I wondered what the worker meant by that statement. I decided to ask about her comment but was interrupted as she announced, "We're here."

We pulled into a long winding street, surrounded by beautiful, two-story homes. All had perfect potted flowers, porch swings and mailboxes that were highlighted with a name and a house number. Once we had made it to the end of the winding street, we approached a dark red brick split level brick house with a two-car garage. This house was surrounded by a white picket fence, petunias, day lilies, and snapdragons.

"O.K. Where are Mr. and Mrs. Dew? There were supposed to be on the front porch to greet us. I will just go ahead and toot my horn."

I found it odd and somewhat disrespectful that she would blow the horn. But sure enough, it worked. The front door opened and out walked a woman and a man that I believed to be, Mr. and Mrs. Dew.

# Chapter 8
## Another Roll of the Dice

Once again, I found myself faced with another roll of the dice. What it really boiled down to was I was expected to trust total strangers who I knew nothing about. My grandmother always told me never to talk to strangers. She also once said strangers can be like the devil as some of them will try and take your soul. I never understood what she meant about that. But I decided it must have been important and there was a lesson behind it. Whether it was right or wrong, that message said there are some people in life who will help you and some who will hurt you.

I knew this stupid home would probably be no different from the others. The rules always reminded me of a clock; as long as I never missed a beat and arrived on time, everything would be fine. I knew today would be no different.

"Hi Lauren, I'm Jane. Welcome to our home. Please, won't you get out and come in?" Before I could respond, I turned to look around for the social worker and Mr. Dew. I wondered why the social worker disappeared so quickly. What happened to Mr. Dew?

"Honey, are you O.K.? You seem a little confused," she said as we walked towards the house.

"Yes ma'am, I'm o.k. I was worried that the social worker left without saying goodbye."

"Now she would never do that. She is inside with Mr. Dew finishing up the paperwork. Look, here they come now."

I quickly turned away from Mrs. Dew only to find the social worker coming out of the house and making her way down the cobblestone steps. Mr. Dew had turned around to go back inside. I began to have "butterfly worries" as I had yet to actually meet Mr. Dew. What could be so important that he had not even said hello?

Was it possible that when the social worker and I arrived in the driveway, Mr. Dew took one look at me and decided I didn't look good enough for him? Before I could give any more thought to Mr. Dew's absence, I was distracted by the cute newspaper delivery guy who nearly crashed into the social worker's car as he tried to start a conversation with me. I must not have been very friendly, because he then peddled away.

I continued to watch the paper boy ride his bike down the dirt path until he faded into a corn field, at which time, I turned around and saw Mr. Dew staring out the front door. I quickly found the social worker to ask if everything was okay.

"Mrs. Jones, why am I still outside? Is there some kind of problem? It's okay if there is. I can always go back to live with Richard."

"Calm down Lauren. Mr. Dew had to finish up some last-minute room changes before you went in. They want you to have the perfect bedroom."

I came so close to calling the social worker a "a big fat liar." That was the dumbest and stupidest excuse I'd ever heard of. Just as I was having second thoughts about calling her a "big fat liar," Mr. Dew walked out.

Mrs. Dew called out to her husband. "Hi Honey, come on and meet Lauren. It's getting late, we need to get her inside and settled into her new room. Can you help out with her bags?"

Mr. Dew responded to his wife with a slightly delayed nod, then made his way towards the car. My heart began to race as I knew this would be our first time to actually say hello. *Should I offer a smile or just act tough? I am so tired of always being the nice guy. I'm not going to do one darn thing.*

"Hi there, I'm here to pick up your suitcases. I am Jane's husband. How many did you bring?"

"Thank you, Mr. Dew. I only brought one brown paper bag, sir. It's not very heavy. I can bring it inside by myself."

"You must not be planning on staying with us very long. But that's okay. too. I will bring it inside the house and put it in the bedroom that you will be visiting."

Before I could respond to Mr. Dew's comments, the social worker interrupted by saying it was time for her to leave.

"I have to go. I have to pick up several other children today. Now Lauren, you are in good hands with Mr. and Mrs. Dew. They have always wanted to have a girl of their own. I'll say goodbye so the three of you can spend time getting to know each other."

Just as Mrs. Jones pulled out of the driveway, a light blue Ford pick-up truck pulled right behind her. By this time, I was making my way up towards the front porch, eager to go inside and finally see my bedroom. However, I noticed that Mrs. Dew had fallen behind, as she was talking to the person who was still sitting in the truck.

I didn't feel comfortable going into the house, as I felt it would be disrespectful to go into anyone's home without permission. I was once mistakenly accused of stealing something from my best friend. I had to collect nasty soda bottles all summer long to pay her back for something I never took. Nope, I was going to wait for Mrs. Dew. All I needed was for Mr. Dew to accuse me of stealing. Mrs. Dew continued to carry on a conversation with this person in the pick-up truck. *Who was this person?*

The conversation all of a sudden got louder. I could hear the voice of a man. It was Mr. Dew in that truck!

I then overheard Jane blurt out. "My God, John, she just got here, and you are running out. Your errand just can't wait until tomorrow? Fine, then just go on. I will explain to Lauren myself. I will get dinner started. We will eat around 6:30. Please be home by then. We need to eat as a family on Lauren's first night with us."

I could hear the desperate pleading, as Jane argued with Mr. Dew. I never heard any response from him. His truck sputtered off down the dirt road spitting up circles of dust down the narrow path. I will never forget the look on Jane's face as she made her way back to the porch area. It was as if she had said her goodbyes to a lover, as he left for war.

Just as Jane approached the front steps, I pretended to be sorting through my bag. "Hi, honey, I am so sorry that I have kept you waiting. I wanted your first day to be so special. Sometimes things don't always work out the way we want them to."

"Yes ma'am, I certainly know what that's all about. Well, what I mean is things have not worked out for me in a very long time."

"Let's go inside and take a look at your new room and get some ice-cold lemonade. Then we can talk for a spell until dinner time. Mr. Dew had to run out to do a few errands. He will be back in time for dinner."

"Wow, you sure do have a pretty home. Who does all the cleaning here? I bet you have a maid."

She answered me as we moved through the house towards my room. "No, I do the cleaning myself. Maybe we can do some cleaning together.

Would you like that? We will have plenty of time to get to know each other over the summer. Right? Now, let's take a look at your room. Close your eyes. In just a few steps you can open them."

"This will be my room? Wow, matching curtains to go with my bedspread. Fresh flowers, too. There is a letter on the desk with my name on it. Is that for me too?"

Yes, why don't you open it?"

This was all too good to be true. Jane was so kind and giving. However, the thought that Mr. Dew would eventually return home haunted me.

"Jane, I don't have a card for you. But I can make up for it by doing some chores around the house. It's such a nice card. No one has ever given me such a special welcome to their home. I feel like I should be giving something to you."

"Now, now, there's an old saying, it's better to give than to receive. So, why don't we just enjoy our time together? I have made up some freshly squeezed lemonade for us so come on let's get a glass."

I took Mrs. Dew up on her offer and slowly followed her down the hallway towards the kitchen. As I cautiously followed behind, I was amazed to find the walls covered with gold-framed photographs of a boy who looked to be at least 15 to 16 years old. There were no pictures of Mr. and Mrs. Dew along the hallway. At the end of the hallway, there was a small brown leather trunk that was padded and locked. On top of the trunk was a candle and a gold key.

My imagination and curiosity were about to get the best of me, as I started to ask Mrs. Dew what was in the trunk? Before I blurted out the question, Mrs. Dew wanted to know if I had changed my mind about the lemonade?

"Yes ma'am, I'm coming. I was just looking at the pictures on the wall." Mrs. Dew never said anything more about the pictures and I took that as "get on to the kitchen and have some lemonade." Once I made my way around the corner, I found Ms. Dew standing over the table with a big smile on her face.

"Okay you can help me pour some lemonade for us. Let's sit for a few minutes and chat before I put the finishing touches on dinner. So, tell me a little about yourself. Do you have brothers and sisters? What do you like to do for fun?"

"Well, there's really not a lot to tell about me that's interesting or funny. Most of the things that I might tell you would either be sad or serious. But I'll tell you some stuff anyway. You seem so easy to talk to. I have four brothers and no sisters. I like to sing in church, and I would like to someday start taking piano lessons. Oh, I am a very good house cleaner. Most people would tell you that I am a very stubborn and strong girl. I am pretty proud of that if you really want to know the truth. What about you?"

"Well honey, I have a husband, a nice home, a job, and I enjoy going to church. I never had a lot of children. I once had a lovely son. Maybe we can talk more after dinner. Would you like to get a little more settled into your room while I finish working on our dinner? Mr. Dew should be home soon. For dinner I have cooked fried chicken, macaroni and cheese, baby lima beans, cold slaw, candied yams, and a home-made apple pie for dessert. I hope that you are hungry."

"You have cooked some of my favorites. I am a bit hungry. I think I will go back to the bedroom and write my brother, Richard, a short letter. Please let me know if I can help out in the kitchen."

My attempts at writing a letter to Richard were distracted by my thoughts that I still needed to talk with Mr. Dew. *What would I talk about with this man? He has already shown his true colors. He is not interested in me. He probably doesn't even want me in his house.*

My thoughts took control, as I must have drifted off to sleep. Suddenly, I was awakened by Jane's gentle touch. While lightly tapping me on my shoulder, she called out my name to let me know that dinner was ready. "Honey, it's later than you think. But it's not too late for you to eat."

"Did I sleep through dinner? If I did, I am so sorry. That is rude and selfish of me to keep you all waiting. I owe Mr. Dew an apology and should tell him in person."

"Honey, it's really okay. Mr. Dew isn't home."

# Chapter 9
# A Sleepless Night

Mrs. Dew and I enjoyed a delicious home cooked meal, and I was enjoying spending time alone with her when she asked me if I was ready for bed, spoiling the moment. My first thought was "dog-gone, she must go to bed with the chickens." That was one of my grandma's favorite sayings that she would often say as she was about to head off to bed. My younger brothers and I would always run around the house like chickens trying to see who could cluck the loudest and would then race to the bedroom to claim the spot next to grandma. I would win every time. Just as I was about to move on to another memory, I was interrupted by Mrs. Dew calling out for me.

Actually, I never completely understood what Grandmother meant about the chickens, but I also knew never to talk back either. So, this night would be no different, only there would no sharing my bed with any chickens. As these good memories passed, the thought of sleeping alone in the Dew's house just didn't feel all that cozy.

"Lauren, aren't you ready for bed? I sure am. I am pretty tired after cooking that big dinner for us."

I wondered why Mr. Dew's weird disappearing act and strange behavior had me on edge? I began to think about ways to keep myself safe in the bedroom just in case Mr. Dew tried to spy on me during the night.

Mrs. Dew called me again, "Lauren, honey, are you O.K? I'm ready for bed. You must be tired too. Why don't we call it a night?"

The clock was now showing 10:00 p.m. and while it still seemed a little too early, I realized I had no say in the matter.

"Yes ma'am. But shouldn't we wait up for Mr. Dew?" I couldn't believe I had asked this question. The truth is I was nosey and wanted more information on his whereabouts.

She never answered me back. I had thought about asking her again, but something told me not to. My grandma told me a long time ago to mind my own business and to always do what grown folks tell you to do. I quickly made my way to the bedroom and got ready for bed.

Just as I was about to climb into bed, there was a soft knocking at my door. "Honey, I wanted to tell you good night. If you need anything, come, and knock on my door. Tomorrow, we will go to church. Would you like that?"

"Yes, Ma'am. My grandma always took me to church. Going to church has always been a part of my life. Good night Mrs. Dew."

Just as Mrs. Dew walked out of my room, I heard the telephone ring. My first thought was "who could be calling so late at night?" My grandma always said, "People who call you late at night are usually calling with bad news or have the wrong number."

But it hit me, maybe it was Mr. Dew calling. Was he hurt? Could he be in hospital? Just for a moment, I felt a little sorry for him. I just had to know what was going on. I quietly got out of my bed and gently cracked opened my door just enough to peak through and hear Mrs. Dew on the phone.

I strained to overhear the conversation she was having on the phone. The conversation became louder, and it was no longer a strain to understand what was being said by Mrs. Dew. I heard Mrs. Dew shout loudly into the phone for Mr. Dew to come home. She later started to beg him by making promises to think about "these decisions." It was at that time I decided I had heard enough. I knew from that moment on that I did not like Mr. Dew.

I returned to my bedroom and kept repeating those words over and over, *these decisions.* What exactly did they mean? My gut feeling is Mr. Dew is not happy with the decision about me coming to their home. His actions had pretty much proven that. It will only be a short period of time before I'll be moving on again. No need to get too cozy up here in this nicely decorated bedroom. It could be here today and gone tomorrow.

I woke the next morning to a familiar smell of breakfast being cooked in the kitchen. My first thought before thinking about leaving my room was "did Mr. Dew make it home last night?" Before I could think any more about my question, I heard his voice.

"Jane, should I go wake up Lauren for breakfast?"

"Yes, honey that would be good. Tell her breakfast is ready."

*Holy cow, he made it home after all.* I didn't want him to come anywhere near me. Not knowing what to do, I decided it would be best to already be awake. That way, he would have no reason to come into my room.

"Lauren, breakfast is ready. It's time to get up."

"Thank you, sir, I am already awake. I will be there in 5 minutes."

As I was getting dressed for breakfast, I felt as if I were going to the dentist to have a tooth pulled. I just didn't want to go. I could make up an excuse and skip breakfast. No, I would not disappoint Mrs. Dew and leave her alone with this man.

Before I was able to greet either Mr. or Mrs. Dew at the breakfast table, Mrs. Dew met me with a morning hug and greeted me.

"Good morning honey, how did you sleep for your first night here?"

I told her I slept well, but before I could add any more details, I was confused, surprised and happy to see that Mr. Dew was missing from the breakfast table. Where could he be now? Speaking of the devil, in walked Mr. Dew with a vase of freshly picked yellow roses.

"Sorry I'm late. I wanted our first breakfast together to be special. So, I picked a few yellow roses for the table."

"Honey, how sweet and thoughtful of you," answered Mrs. Dew.

The flowers were pretty, but the man was ugly. It took me a minute to find the right words to offer to Mr. Dew for bringing the flowers to breakfast.

"Mr. Dew those yellow roses remind me of a poem that I learned in elementary school. It goes like this. Roses are red, violets are blue; can we plant some in the zoo?"

I wasn't particularly proud of this poem but figured it was all he deserved. The rest of the time spent that morning at the breakfast table felt awkward, as Mr. Dew pretty much ignored me and talked about his plans for the day with Mrs. Dew. Just as I was about to ask to be excused Mrs. Dew announced, "It's time to get ready for church."

"Lauren, you go ahead and start getting ready and I'll clear the table."

"I don't mind helping with the dishes first and then get dressed."

"Maybe next time. We are running a little behind schedule and need to leave in 30 minutes. I don't want you to have to rush in getting ready on your first day."

Going to church was something I always looked forward to. My grandma believed that every time the church doors were opened, a parent should have their children there. During summer months, our church had Vacation Bible School for children to attend and this was one of my favorite activities for kids that the church provided. Church was also a place for families to go to when they needed help with food and sometimes money to help pay for rent. Growing up poor, it was a blessing to have support from our church to help with food and other important matters.

"Honey, are you almost ready?"

I had not given much thought about what I would wear to church and here at the last minute, I realized I had searched through the brown paper bag three times for something to wear and each time, I came up with nothing. I began to panic. What was I going to do? I can't go to church with Mrs. Dew looking like an orphan child. Just as I was about to fake a horrible stomachache, there was a knock at my door.

"Lauren, can I come in? I have something for you. I bought you a brand-new outfit. I thought that you might want to wear it to church."

Fumbling for words, "Yes, Ma'am. I love it. It is so pretty. I can really wear it today?"

"Yes, now hurry and put it on. We have to leave in 5 minutes."

That was the prettiest dress I had ever owned. It was a lavender print with a lace collar. How did she know my size? Once I finished dressing with my hair combed all into place, I felt like a million dollars. I wondered if Mrs. Dew would allow me to keep this dress. Then a little voice told me: *Just be happy for today, and don't worry about tomorrow.* I took one last look in the mirror, smiled at myself, and dashed out the door to meet Mrs. Dew.

# Chapter 10
# Sunday Blues

Growing up, I often saw church as a "home away from home." It was a place that was safe, fun, and sometimes even a way to get a free meal. Now don't get me wrong, I was never a person to beg or have others feel sorry for me. I would be more likely to leave hungry or be the first to raise my hand to give away my serving from a Wednesday night's cover dish event to an elder member. There were many activities the church provided for children. Two of my favorites were vacation bible school and the Christmas play.

One particular summer during vacation bible school, we were encouraged to invite other friends to attend with the incentive of a prize for whoever could invite the most friends. I had made up my mind that I wanted to win this contest. I don't remember what the prize was. I went around the neighborhood and invited all the kids to join me on a free vacation where they could eat good food, make arts and crafts, and play games. By the end of the day, I had signed up 10 kids from the neighborhood.

The next day, however, I ran into a little problem as these kids never showed up at church. I later found out that the parents thought I had played a joke on the kids by inviting them to go on a vacation. Later that week, I gave an apology to every kid's parent and asked if they would think about coming to vacation bible school's final activity which was a cake and ice-cream party. Some of the parents agreed to bring their kids, but there were still a few parents who turned down the offer.

In many ways, church filled my summer days. However, it was about this time in my life that I learned all good things come to an end. As my mother's mental health began to take a turn for the worse, my church going days became fewer and fewer.

The days that I would go, the guilt would drive away any fun that I might find there. So, when I stayed at home, I tried to keep my mind busy by daydreaming, thinking about having better days.

Now in this foster home, I figured that daydreaming would get me through again, but just as I was finishing up with one daydream and before I could think up another, I heard my name.

"Lauren?" It was Mrs. Dew; she was calling me.

"Honey, are you ready to go?"

"Yes, Ma'am, I'm coming."

"So, how are you feeling about going to a new church today?"

"I'm O.K. Why are you asking me that question?"

"Honey, I'm just checking on you."

"I guess I'm not used to people just checking on me. I mean, most of the time, people don't really care."

"Well, I do care. Now, today, I want you to stay close by me. This is a big church with lots of people. I don't want you to feel uncomfortable. Also, some of these ladies can be a little nosey and may try to ask you a lot of questions that just ain't any of their business."

"Yes ma'am. But I'm not scared of big churches or any kind of people, big or small. I will have answers to their questions, so please don't worry about me."

"Honey, just trust me, I want to take care of you and protect you."

"O.K. But I am pretty strong and tough. Oh, what about the children who go to this church? Are they nosey too? Should I talk to them?"

"Honey, just for today, I want you to stick close by me. I will introduce you to a few people. So, relax, everything will be O.K."

The rest of the ride to church was fairly quiet. There were still several questions that continued to dance around in my head. One was Mrs. Dew getting cold feet and having second thoughts about me? Did she think she made a mistake about bringing me to her church? Why all of a sudden was she being so controlling and worried? I supposed only time would tell, as we finally arrived at the church.

"We're here," Mrs. Dew announced. "My, the parking lot is full. We will never find a parking spot. Oh, I see one right by Sister June's car."

"Wow, it is a big church. But it doesn't scare me at all."

"O.K. then, let's be quick, the service begins in less than 5 minutes."

At a fairly young age, I learned that fear was something you must face and never run from. That way of thinking gave me strength and courage to face situations that otherwise I may not have been able to. This day would be no different, as I would be walking into a new church, perhaps meeting people who might or might not like me. Once we were out of the car, Mrs. Dew took my hand and cradled it inside hers.

Just as we walked inside the church, the preacher was standing at the pulpit already making an announcement to welcome all new visitors. I am not sure if it was my imagination or not, but it felt as if all eyes were on me. I thought Mrs. Dew would never find a place for us to sit. I wanted to scream, *would you just sit down, and stop drawing attention by looking for the perfect pew*. Finally, she found a place that was next to some lady who stared me up and down as I cautiously moved past her to take my seat.

The preacher continued the service with the usual routine of singing, passing of the offering plate, praying, and reading of the Bible. At one time during the service, two elderly women who were sitting a pew in front of us went out of their way to catch a glimpse of me and Mrs. Dew. The looks that came from these women were pretty scary. I wished the preacher would have caught a glimmer of this Jezabel's disgusting look. My grandmother would tell these women, "This is God's house and you do not disrespect him in his own house."

The service finally ended. I looked over and saw Mrs. Dew talking to the woman who eye-balled us when we sat down. There was nothing I could do but wait, as I had no desire to talk to anyone.

"Honey let's go out front so I can introduce you to a few of my lady friends. They are waiting for us."

"Yes, Ma'am."

As we made our way out of the church, I caught a glimpse of a few kids who appeared to be around my age. I had a funny feeling that they were not really interested in me, as they quickly became interested in another girl's conversation. It was no skin of my back, as I really didn't want to be bothered by the kids anyway.

"Lauren, come on. Mrs. Gertrude wants to meet you."

"Mrs. Gertrude, this is Lauren, she is living with us now."

"Oh, really? Well, hello Lauren. How are you?"

"Hello Mrs. Gertrude. I'm fine. Thank you."

Mrs. Gertrude continued, "Jane, honey, I have to go. I have dinner to prepare for my oldest daughter and son-in-law."

"O.k. Well, isn't Lauren adorable?"

Mrs. Gertrude replied, "She seems interesting."

I could tell that Mrs. Gertrude really didn't have much to say about me. In some ways, she was no different from some of the social workers that I had been around in the past. They would say just enough to get by. That day in the parking lot, I could see the disappointment in Mrs. Dew's eye, as Mrs. Gertrude walked away. It hurt me more for Mrs. Dew than for myself.

"Lauren, honey I need to run and pick-up a cake plate from the church kitchen. Do you want to come along or sit in the car? It will only take five minutes or so."

"I would rather wait in the car."

"I promise I will be back in a jiffy and then we'll head home for a delicious home cooked Sunday meal."

Just as I was settled into a calm relaxed state, I heard a "tap, tap, tap" on the car window. I looked up and saw that it was a girl about my age motioning for me to roll down the glass. I felt safe enough being in the car, so I went ahead and opened the window.

"Hi, my name is Elizabeth. I heard about you living with Mr. and Mrs. Dew."

I thought it was strange that she started the conversation with that comment. I had a funny feeling about her.

"Yes, I am living with them. They are nice." I should have said Mrs. Dew was nice.

"How long will you live with them?"

There she went again with another stupid-ass question. *I'm sorry God. Here I am on your property saying bad words. Please forgive me.*

"Why do you want to know?"

"I was just curious."

"Haven't you ever heard that old saying, 'curiosity killed the cat?'"

That must have been the wrong thing to say, as Elizabeth froze and remained silent for at least thirty seconds. During that time, I thought, "where is Mrs. Dew?"

"I really don't like jokes like that." Elizabeth came back at me.

"I'm sorry if I upset you."

"Well, there's something that I bet you haven't ever heard of. I also bet that it will upset you."

"Well, it takes a lot to upset me and not much can hurt me these days. So, I guess you will just have to try."

"O.K. You asked for it. The real reason that the Dews got you to live with them is because their son died. He burned up in his very own car. It happened just around the corner. Now, how does that make you feel?"

"You are a liar. I don't believe any of what you just said. You are a big fat liar."

Just as I began to get louder and louder, Mrs. Dew approached the car. Elizabeth took off running and I rolled up the car window.

"Honey, I am so sorry that I was gone so long. It looks like you met Elizabeth."

"Yes, ma'am."

"So, what were you all talking about?"

"Nothing really, just about things we liked."

*Could it be true? Did Mrs. Dew's son burn to death in his own car? Did she ask for me, as a way to try and replace her son? How will I ever learn the answers to these questions?*

# Chapter 11
# Two's Company and Three's a Crowd

Driving home from church, Mrs. Dew and I barely spoke. The silence between us grew more uncomfortable. I didn't know what to do. I never believed in the old saying "silence is golden." One of my worst childhood memories was when people gave me the "silent treatment." My best friend, Sarah in first grade, told me that the "silent treatment" was given to people who were losers, not winners. I believed my best friend because her father was a Southern Baptist preacher, and she was a born-again Christian who was raised to never tell a lie. Shortly after the welfare people separated me from my family, I noticed others giving me the silent treatment on a fairly regular basis.

The silent treatment often felt like a punishment. Just as I expected to face another silent treatment on our drive home following church service, I heard my name called.

"Lauren…Honey…I am sorry that I haven't been much of a talker today. I have been…Huh…. Well, it's too hard for me to explain it to you. I will tell you that today is a special day, but also a sad day for me."

"What do you mean? How can a day be special and sad at the same time?"

"I told you; I don't know how to tell you. I don't want to confuse you or hurt you."

"Please tell me. I am stronger than you think. Nothing really hurts me anymore. I really don't like getting the silent treatment from people. So, you can tell me anything you want to."

Before I could say anymore, Mrs. Dew quickly pulled the car off to the side of the road and began to cry. I didn't know how to respond. Should I be strong and just let her cry? Things didn't feel quite right, as I just sat there doing nothing. Finally, I thought of something I could do. I noticed lying in the middle console of the car was a small black leather King James Version Bible. I picked up the Bible and flipped through the pages searching for the only scripture that I learned from my grandmother Byrd. It was the 23rd Psalm.

I read aloud, "The Lord is my Shepard, I shall not want..." I must have read halfway through the verse when I felt Mrs. Dew reach over and take hold of my hand.

"Thank you honey for being so kind. I am going to tell you about a special person that I love very much. Two years ago, my sweet boy, Eddie Jr., was killed in a car wreck. I miss him so much. Today is the third-year anniversary of his death."

"Mrs. Dew, I am so sorry. I didn't know. I wish I could make you feel better. What I mean is, I know that I'm not the same as Eddie, but I can be a pretty good girl and make you happy."

"It's okay honey. You are so sweet. Someday, you will be treasured by someone very special. I hope that day comes very soon for you."

It was at that moment I knew my days were numbered living with the Dews. It would probably be only a matter of time before the welfare case worker made a visit to break the news that it was time to pack my bags and move on to different pastures.

I had also made my mind up that it was not worth it to ask any more questions. It was a "done deal" as my brothers used to say when we would trade our marbles back and forth knowing that once we made a deal, there was no looking back. But just for a few moments, I thought, wait a minute, this is not about trading or getting rid of marbles, it's about getting rid of me. Why does any of this matter, I thought? I'm supposed to be tough, strong, and able to walk away from pain. But this go around isn't so easy.

"Lauren…Lauren…Honey, are you okay.?"

"Yes, ma'am. I am fine."

I hope I haven't said anything that has upset you.

"No, I am great."

"Okay. Why don't we do something special? I have an idea. How would you like to stop at the Tastee Freeze for a juicy cheeseburger, fries, and soda pop?"

"I love cheeseburgers. Could we really do that? Should we get something for Mr. Dew? He needs to eat lunch too."

"We can always get some hot dogs for him. He will be fine."

What a relief I felt to not have to face Mr. Dew for another painful face-to-face sit-down meal. I'd almost rather eat a can of red beets (my least favorite food in the world) than eat another meal with that man.

Mrs. Dew forewarned me that on Sundays, a person could stand in line at the Tastee Freeze for over 30 minutes before ordering their food. However, she reminded me the food would be well worth the wait. Today was no exception. We stood in line for 35 minutes and then decided to take our food back to the car because all the picnic benches had been taken.

There was very little conversation between eating our cheeseburgers and sharing the banana split. We both were starving. However, I still had questions about the death of Mrs. Dew's son but decided today was not the day to ask them. The short drive home from the Tastee Freeze was mostly chit chat about things to do during the coming week.

Just as we pulled into the driveway, Mr. Dew appeared from the house, took a seat on the front steps, and lit up a cigarette. I couldn't believe what I was seeing. I turned to Mrs. Dew and said, "I didn't know that Mr. Dew smoked cigarettes."

After the car rolled to a stop, Mrs. Dew reached back to collect her belongings from the back seat of the car. She then caught sight of Mr. Dew puffing away on his cigarette.

"What is he doing?" Mrs. Dew remarked.

"Ma'am, he is smoking a cigarette." Obviously, she had not heard me the first time.

"I know that! Has he lost his mind?" Mrs. Dew jerked the car door open and leapt onto the driveway running while shouting, "Why are you smoking? You told me you quit 6 months ago. You lied to me!"

I was too afraid to leave the car and decided to just wait out the storm. Once Mr. and Mrs. Dew left the front porch and made their way to the back yard, I ran as fast as I could into the house to hide out in my room. Things became calm surprisingly fast. There were no signs of arguing or bickering. Still, something didn't seem right. Rather, as my grandmother would say, something felt "fishy."

The events of the day had worn me out. I thought I should think about something happy to push back the sadness, but I wasn't getting the bad thoughts out of my mind. Fortunately, I was surprised by a knock at my door.

"Honey, I need to talk to you for a moment," said Mrs. Dew.

"Yes, Ma'am."

"I am going out for about 45 minutes. I will be back. I have called Mrs. Jones next door to have her look in on you while I am gone. Do you feel okay about that?"

"Sure. I'm not afraid of anything. I will be fine. Don't you worry about me."

"Of course, I worry about you. Now, when I come back, we can decide what we want to have for dinner tonight."

"Okay, I have plenty of things to do while you're gone."

Just as Mrs. Dew was walking out the door, she turned back into my room as if she had forgotten something. "Honey, before I forget, I need to tell you that there will be a social worker from the Welfare Department visit us tomorrow at 11:00 a.m."

"Okay." What I really wanted to say was "Should I have my bags packed and ready to go?"

# Chapter 12
## Some Changes Ain't that Bad

In the back of my mind, I always knew Mr. Dew would have the final word. I learned very early during my childhood that there are winners and losers. But I also remembered that in the end, only one person would find the golden egg. It didn't matter how strong, determined, or stubborn I was, I knew that I stood no chance of being recognized as the winner for finding a golden egg, let alone finding a secure home at the Dews. My gut feeling told me it was only a matter of time, that I would be packing my bags and moving on.

There has been only a hand full of times in my life that I have walked away from an unfair situation without a good fight. One of those times occurred when I decided to compete in the Halloween carnival queen contest in second grade. This was a contest that I knew would be a tough win because it was all about money. The truth was my family had no money. However, this still didn't change the fact that I was determined to find a way to win the contest because I knew I was not a quitter.

I didn't win, but I didn't lose. I was awarded 2$^{nd}$ runner-up. The winner turned out to be a skinny little first grade girl who lived in my neighborhood and had a rich daddy. I knew that she won the contest fair and square. I decided to suck it up and be happy for both of us. I also knew this would be what my grandmother would want me to do.

I never thought of myself as a "Miss. Goodie Two Shoes." Most of my life, I have put others first and settled for leftovers. My grandmother taught me many life lessons. The one that I have struggled with since the loss my family is "Do unto others as you would have others do unto you."

All of this was running through my mind as I slowly realized my time at the Dews was probably coming to an end. Before I went to bed that night, I had decided there was no reason to "pussy-foot around" as my grandmother would often tell me, so I found my brown paper bag and packed up my clothes to be ahead of their game. As I lay in bed that night, I wondered if Mrs. Dew would be sad about my leaving or if she might miss me. There have been times throughout my early childhood when I wished I could read people's minds. However, if my grandmother were here, she would remind me that sometimes you need to be careful about what you wish for because it might come true. I finally accepted that it was useless to sugar-coat this situation because it was a "done deal."

I tossed and turned for several hours until I finally dozed off into a light sleep. My last night sleeping at the Dew's home was filled with frightening dreams about Mr. Dew and his plan to hurt me before I left. I later thought of these dreams as a sign that it was meant for me to leave this place. Somehow, I managed to steal about four hours of sleep before I heard a knock on my door telling me breakfast was ready.

I quickly replied to let Mrs. Dew know that I was almost dressed and would join her in five minutes. I had no interest or desire to have a "one-on-one moment" with Mrs. Dew that morning. Somehow, I had convinced myself that time alone with Mrs. Dew would set me up for showing emotions of weakness and sadness. This was not a time for weakness, rather a time for strength and courage. At the last minute before I exited the bedroom for breakfast, I grabbed my brown bag of belongings. I had no desire to return to a bedroom that would no longer be mine.

Before I made it to the breakfast table, I overheard Mrs. Dew ending a conversation with someone on the telephone. I decided to give her privacy and lingered in the hallway for a few seconds before making my appearance. It was at that time, I heard her say, "Honey, are you almost ready? You don't have to dress up. It's only going to be you and me for breakfast."

I thought to myself "Hum, Mr. Dew isn't joining us? Yippee!" For a moment, I felt that my appetite might just return.

Mrs. Dew had prepared enough food for a small army. The table was covered with silver-dollar blueberry pancakes, spiced apples, fresh strawberries, bran muffins, orange juice and hot maple syrup. Our conversation throughout breakfast was different from other breakfast talks. This particular morning, we only had small talk. I wasn't born yesterday, another one of my grandmother's sayings, and I was well aware of how Mrs. Dew didn't seem herself.

The doorbell rang before the breakfast dishes had been cleared from the table. I had already made up my mind that I was not going to answer the door, even though I knew Mrs. Dew had gone out back to pick some flowers. I continued to tidy up the kitchen and began to make my way back to the bedroom when I heard the doorbell ring again. Then, immediately following the sound of the doorbell, I heard three loud bangs on the door.

Darn it, where is she? I said I wasn't going to answer that dang door. I even made a cross and spit on it as a promise on my grandmother's grave not to answer the cotton-picking door. Well, so much for keeping promises. Before I could reach the door, there came louder knocks. I jerked open the door and blurted out, "It's open!"

"Excuse *me*," said the woman. I am here to meet with Mrs. Dew and…" Before she could even get my name out, Mrs. Dew appeared and rescued me from that uncomfortable moment. She apologized for not hearing the doorbell and shared with this woman that she had been busy out back cutting fresh flowers.

Mrs. Dew then warmly welcomed her into the house.

"Lauren, honey have you introduced yourself to Mrs. Peabody?"

"Well not exactly. I just opened the door for her."

"It's really not important," interrupted Mrs. Peabody. "We really need to get started with our meeting. We have a lot of information to talk about and decisions to make. So, where should we sit to have our meeting?"

Mrs. Dew quickly suggested that we gather around the kitchen table where she later offered to serve ice-cold tea and coffee. Mrs. Peabody was not interested in having any chit-chat, as she seemed to be a woman on a mission with a plan. Mrs. Peabody, without hesitation or permission, started the discussion about the plans for my future.

She read from a list of notes, "Lauren, you will no longer be able to live with Mr. and Mrs. Dew. We will need to find you a new home." She also added that this had been a "business decision." Mrs. Peabody also found it in her heart to tell me that this decision had been a hard one for Mr. and Mrs. Dew to make.

I still could not believe that things would end this way. What happened to my special friend Mrs. Dew? She was supposed to be different from the others. Why didn't she speak up for me? In the back of my mind, I was frightened that Mr. Dew had in some way threatened her and was behind the plans for giving me back to Social Services.

Mrs. Peabody continued the meeting by allowing me to choose between living in an orphanage or with another family. She also made it very clear that all future plans would not include living with my brothers. It was at that time I learned that my brothers' future had already been decided. They had been adopted together by the same family.

For me it became a "no-brainer." I wasn't going to a darn stupid orphanage home. I figured that if I were tucked away in some orphanage, it would end all hope of me ever finding my brothers again. I was getting pretty used to the routine of "musical homes." At the same time, I continued to daydream about going to a perfect home where I felt that I belonged. My hope was to find a family who wanted to take me because I deserved a home. A decision that left no doubts and was not based on money.

The meeting ended with the decision that I would settle for another home placement over an orphanage. However, Mrs. Peabody provided both me and Mrs. Dew with some interesting information about my new placement. She shared that the new family wanted to invite me for a weekend visit before I made my final decision about staying. I agreed to the weekend visit.

The timing of my leaving the Dews' home could not have been any more perfect. Mr. Dew had planned to take 2 weeks of vacation next week, which meant he would be home. Having me around would surely interfere and make for a disappointing time off. My leaving would make a more enjoyable vacation for him. Mrs. Peabody gave me the option to leave for the weekend visit after our meeting, or she could return in the late afternoon. It was totally out of the question that I would spend another night under the same roof with that man, Mr. Dew. This would not be a business decision. It would now change to a personal decision. My decision!

My separation from the Dews' home was quick and painless. There was no lingering or time to feel sad or to say things I might regret. There are some things that just aren't meant to be. Sometimes in life, changes really ain't all that bad. Yes, this would be one of those times and one of those "God's Blessing" changes.

# Chapter 13
# The Grass May be Greener on the Other Side

It was truly an answer to prayer that I did not spend another night in the Dew's home. To be honest, I probably would have done something really stupid, like run away or spit out a few nasty words to Mr. Dew that I may have regretted later.

Grandmother once heard me shout out one of these words as a child when I called my brother a "stupid shit head." To teach me a lesson, my grandmother made me go out in the backyard and pick my favorite switch from a green thorny bush so she could beat me for using the devil's words.

Well, in the end, I didn't run away, I didn't curse out Mr. Dew and I didn't look back. I left the Dews that afternoon with my head held high, no tears and no fears. There was no going away party or apologies. It was just an ordinary day. Perhaps the best part of the day was that the social worker surprised us all by showing up two hours early.

Once we were in the car and ready to pull out of the driveway, I thought to myself, I don't even know this lady's name. For some reason, I didn't care. I mean after all; she should be in charge and do her job. After thinking for about 30 seconds, I quickly changed my mind and wanted to know about my next new home. But before I started to ask my first question, she spoke.

"So, Miss Lauren, tell me about you. What do you like to do for fun?"

"I'm sorry, but I don't even know your name."

"Oh dear. I am so sorry. You can call me Mrs. Peabody, dear. Didn't I introduce myself?"

"No ma'am."

"So, go ahead, tell me a little about yourself. Then I will tell you about me and my grandchildren."

"Well, Mrs. Peabody there's really not much to tell. To be honest with you, my stuff isn't very exciting or important. But, Mrs. Peabody, I do need to ask you about this new home that I'm going to. Can you tell me about it? Please."

"Sweetheart, it sounds like you don't want to talk about yourself. It's Okay. You seem like a sweet and smart girl. Sure, I can tell you a little about your new home. What would you like to know?"

"Tell me about the family. Will there be a girl there my age?"

"Hum, I did read the case notes and remember the family's name is Mr. and Mrs. Brown. The family has one daughter who is 11 yrs. old. Mrs. Brown works as a schoolteacher and Mr. Brown works as an administrator. I remember reading in my notes that this family enjoys going camping and to the beach during the summer. So, what do you think?"

"I'm not sure. I guess they sound okay. They sound important and rich. But I am glad that there will be a girl who is my age. Do you know her name?"

"Yes, I forgot to tell you that. Her name is Glenda."

"That sounds nice. Uh, why would this family want another girl when they already have one?"

"I'm not sure. There could be many reasons. My, you seem to worry a lot for someone your age. What's that all about?"

*Lady, you wouldn't believe me if I told you. Besides, even if I trusted you, it might sound like I'm a weakling. You might even think I wanted you to feel sorry for me. Let me tell you, that ain't what I want from you or anyone in this crazy old world.*

"Mrs. Peabody, you are a really nice lady. But the truth is, I haven't had a lot of luck growing up as a child. Maybe someday my luck will change. For now, I will just keep plugging away and never give up."

"My, you are one strong little girl. This family will surely be happy to have you live with them."

*Yeah, just like all the other families? Only time would tell the tale, as my grandmother would put it when she didn't believe I was telling the truth.*

"Well, Mrs. Peabody, I will just have to keep my fingers crossed. Most families either didn't care very much for me or got tired of having me around."

"That just can't be. I have never heard any such thing in my life," said Mrs. Peabody.

"Honey, you don't deserve such treatment from anyone."

"Mrs. Peabody, don't you know that life ain't always fair? Can we talk about something else?"

"Sure, we can. What would you like to talk about?"

"Can you tell me about your family? Do you have any children?"

"Well, I really don't know very much about my birth family. I grew up in an orphanage home. This is a special home for children who do not have parents. But I did make a family of my own and now I have two grandchildren."

*Hum, is she telling me the truth? Maybe she is making up this story, so I won't feel so bad. Well, she is a little nice to me. Maybe she is telling the truth.*

"Mrs. Peabody, I am sorry. Were you sad growing up?"

"That was so long ago, it's hard to remember. But I do remember always being strong and wanting to help others."

"Is that why you grew up and decided to be a social worker?"

"Maybe. Why don't we talk about something that tastes good? Maybe like ice cream! Would you like to stop for an ice-cream cone?"

"Yes ma'am, I would like that."

# Chapter 14
# Home Sweet Home

Mrs. Peabody had promised to take me to a very special store. It was known for the most famous banana split float in the south. Unfortunately, we found it had gone out of business. Surprisingly, Mrs. Peabody did not handle disappointing news very well. You would have thought she was the child and me the adult. Of course, I wanted an ice-cream cone on that day, but to be honest, it wasn't the end of the world if I didn't get an ice cream cone. Perhaps we would find another place to stop before reaching my new home. The disappointment of the ice cream store being closed brought on little to talk about.

Mrs. Peabody eventually broke the silence, "Well, there is one other place that sells soft serve ice-cream that's only about 15 minutes away. There is a hot dog stand in the next county that also sells ice cream. The only problem is the best flavors sell out fast."

I asked, "What is your favorite flavor?"

"It is definitely strawberry. What about yours?"

"Well, it's not all that exciting, but it's vanilla. My brothers once gave me the nickname 'plain Jane' because many of the foods I ate were pretty boring. You know, food like plain grits, mayonnaise sandwiches, fish roe, tuna fish right out of the can and raw bacon."

"Well, honey, if you like that kind of food, then you like it. It's the same thing about ice cream, if vanilla is your favorite flavor, then vanilla is what we will get you. Besides, we all know boys will be boys. Now honey, that's just an old saying. I am not saying anything mean about your brothers. O.K.?"

"I know all about that saying. I also know that you are not a mean person."

We found the hot dog stand and we both enjoyed a cup of our favorite ice-cream. There was no time for any chit-chat because we were trying to arrive at the Brown's home by 4:00 p.m. The last thing I needed was to ruffle any feathers by showing up late. I also knew this could be a "do or die" moment. This could be my last chance to have a home to live in rather than an orphanage home.

"Lauren, we are almost there. I must have read the directions wrong because the road sign says we are 5 miles to Gillespie Street. So, we will be a little early."

"Will being early be a bad thing?"

"No, honey. It will be a good thing. Honey, are you worried?"

"Well… I guess I am a bit nervous, but I am not scared. I believe these two feelings are different. I even looked in the dictionary for these two words and saw that the meanings were different."

"Yes, honey I understand that you may feel nervous. It will be O.K. I promise."

I never told Mrs. Peabody that I also felt sad. I knew that I would probably never see her again and she would forget about me. Maybe I could write her letters to let her know how I am doing. In many ways, I wished I could live with Mrs. Peabody.

"We have almost arrived. The next street is Gillespie."

For the next five minutes, my eyes stayed focused on the road. I knew it was best not to look at Mrs. Peabody because this was not a time for weakness. I had to be strong, once again. The car finally turned onto the road that I might soon be calling my home. There were only a few houses on this street. We had passed every house except for the last one ahead. The last house on the left had to be the one. It was the biggest house on the street and had the biggest yard. My first thought was this must be the richest family in the neighborhood.

Next, I noticed a big light green Cadillac parked in front of a mustard yellow house with a wrap-around porch. Once Mrs. Peabody had the car parked in front of the house, I had these flashbacks of Mr. and Mrs. Dew. I guess in some ways, I was scared that Mr. and Mrs. Brown could be another nightmare. Just as I was about to have another painful memory, the front door opened and there stood a man and a girl about my age.

This man looked nothing like Mr. Dew, nor did he look particularly happy to see me. Oh boy, here we go again. The girl leaped off the porch almost tripping over one of the rocking chairs as she ran out to the car to greet us. Mrs. Peabody and I were already out of the car before the girl was face to face with us.

"Hi, I'm Glenda. You must be Lauren?"

"Yes. Hi, Glenda, it's nice to meet you."

"Hi, Glenda. I'm Mrs. Peabody. Is your mom or dad home?"

"Uh, yeh, my dad is up on the porch. I guess he is still waiting for my mom to come out."

Mrs. Peabody and I both turned from Glenda to the front porch to Mr. Brown, but there was no sign of him. Before anyone could say anything, the front door opened. Mr. and Mrs. Brown walked out and approached the three of us in the driveway.

"Hello, I am Mrs. Peabody, and this is Lauren."

"Hi, Lauren. Welcome to your new home. We are so happy to have you." Mrs. Brown spoke. Mr. Brown remained silent.

"Hey, me too," added Glenda.

"Thank you," I responded in a polite but cautious way.

Glenda picked up the conversation, "Hey, Lauren, I have so much to show you about our house. I can't wait."

"Honey don't rush Lauren," interrupted her mother, "we have to get all of her clothes and things out of the car first. Then, we want to help her settle in her room and maybe have a snack before y'all start roaming around."

"Lauren, I don't mind getting your things from the car for you," spoke Mr. Brown for the first time.

I must have wandered off into some far away land still thinking about Mr. Dew. My thoughts were interrupted, and I was startled by Mrs. Peabody's voice, "Honey, Mr. Brown offered to help with your bag."

"Oh. Yes, sir. That would be nice. I really don't have very much stuff for you to carry."

Glenda jumped in with a question, "Dang, why didn't you bring all your stuff? I thought you were coming to live with us?"

"Well, I did bring everything. Why don't I just bring my own things inside? Glenda, would you mind showing me inside?"

# Chapter 15
# Now Why Am I Here?

For the first few weeks at the Browns, I felt like I was on summer vacation. Glenda and I were two peas in a pod. We spent a lot of time getting to know each other. We rode bikes, went swimming, listened to her entire record collection of the Bay City Rollers and Paul Anka, and went roller skating on the weekends. This kind of fun and lifestyle was something I had read about but never dreamed I would ever be a part of.

By the time summer came to an end, Glenda and I developed a friendship. We learned a lot about each other's hopes, dreams, and fears. At the same time, we ran into a few differences. But when it was all said and done, we worked it out and still liked each other. The one difference between us that was the most disappointing was our taste in clothing. Glenda was a "tomboy" and would not be caught dead wearing a dress. Playing "dress up" was a childhood activity I liked. There was something magical about wearing dresses. I found 'dressing up" as a way to feel special and pretty.

Wearing dresses, at times, got me attention and an occasional compliment. I never had very many people in my life tell me what I looked like, be it pretty or ugly. I decided one day to take a chance by asking a stranger if they thought I looked pretty in my dress. The answer that I got back was I looked like a sweet little sack girl. I wished I had never asked that question. My grandmother gets all the credit for my love of dresses. She always reminded me that wearing dresses was pleasing to God. I never knew exactly what my grandmother meant by saying that. However, I trusted my grandmother and always wanted to please her.

I truly believed and honored many of the beliefs and values of my grandmother, I was still a curious, stubborn, and courageous child who was never afraid to test the water. I once had a babysitter whose job was to sit for one of the foster families where I had been temporarily placed.

This sitter took care of us on several occasions and had taken a liking to me. In many ways, she showed me favoritism over all the other children.

I decided I was going to ask her if she thought I was pretty. I knew I would be taking a risk by asking this question. I also knew what my grandmother's advice would be, "be careful what you ask for." She also told me to always make sure that you're able to handle the answer to a question. On that day, I thought I was ready and willing to accept the answer from this babysitter. But I guess I had fooled myself because when I heard, "Well, I guess you look O.K." I realized I didn't like the answer I got.

Since that day, I promised myself that I would never rely on other's opinions, as I would likely be disappointed. Living with the Browns, I found myself constantly worrying about how I looked. My self-doubt was always about being too fat, over-eating and not being smart enough.

As the summer months ended, I realized that the past two months of fun and excitement had been centered around Glenda leaving me with minimal interaction with the Browns. In many ways, I knew very little about the Browns and they knew little about me. In the back of mind, I told myself it was only a matter of time before the Browns would reach out and want to know more about me.

The beginning of fall brought about many new beginnings, adventures, and struggles. This would be my first year starting Junior High as well as going to a new school. For some strange reason, I had dreamed about the day in which I would be a junior high girl. I suppose a lot of this excitement was about my crazy thoughts that I might be able to wear high-heel shoes rather than the usual boring flats. The truth of the matter is that never happened. First of all, I didn't own any such shoes and even if I did, I wouldn't have the nerve to wear them around Mrs. Brown.

I had only two days left before school started. I began to worry about the clothes I had to wear. The few clothes that I had were not pretty. I guess even worse than that, I realized that I only had 3 sets of clothes. The last thing that I needed was to embarrass Glenda and worry about being picked on. I had to come up with a plan on how to get some clothes.

Maybe I'm jumping the gun. Should I wait for Mrs. Brown to surprise me with new school clothes? I know what I should do; I will ask Glenda about our school clothes. She will have the answers. I waited for Glenda to return home that afternoon to ask her about any plans for us being able to buy new school clothes. As I was about to look through the few pieces of clothes that I owned, someone was knocking at my door.

"It's open. Come on in." The door opened and there stood Mr. Brown just staring at me. After feeling uneasy and awkward, I broke the silence. "Hi Mr. Brown. How are you?"

"I just wanted to see how you're doing. Let me know if you need anything."

"Thank you, Mr. Brown. That is nice of you to offer. But I am doing O.K. Do you know when Glenda is coming home?"

"I think she should be home anytime."

"Thank you, Mr. Brown."

When Mr. Brown left my room, there was something about him that seemed strange and almost a little scary. The feeling that he left with me was "lock your door, Lauren." Once Glenda got home that afternoon, I found her and asked about our school clothes. I found out that Mrs. Brown doesn't believe in paying high prices for clothes or other items around the time of special occasions or events. She only shops during sales events and at thrift/second-hand stores. Glenda also told me that we would get our school clothes one week after school started.

"Didn't my mom tell you all this stuff?"

"No."

"She probably forgot to tell you. Don't worry; she will talk to you about it."

"O.K. But, Glenda, do you think I could borrow one or two outfits from you until we get some clothes?"

"Sure, you can. But you ain't going to find no dresses hanging up in my closet."

"That's O.K. I just thank you for helping me out."

I never had that official conversation with Mrs. Brown about getting school clothes. I wasn't surprised or mad, as the more I was around Mrs. Brown, I got a funny feeling about her.

The first two weeks of school I hated. I had no new clothes, received free lunch and everyone referred to me as "Glenda's foster sister." Every day, I was stopped by either a student or a nosey teacher and was confronted with questions such as, "Are you an orphan? Why did your parents leave you? Did your parents die or beat you?" One day after I could not bear to hear any more questions, I lost my patience and screamed out, "Have you lost your cotton-picking-mind... you do-do-bird brain?" Well, it later turned out, I had screamed out this message to the assistant principal, Mrs. Irene. She barely looked to be much older than some of the students.

That particular day I got to know Mrs. Irene pretty well, as I spent half the day down in her office telling her all about me. The assistant principal and I became pretty close that year. Later in the year, I learned she grew up in an orphanage home and we connected in many ways.

The best part of the school year was trying out for the cheerleading team with Glenda. This was exciting but scary at the same time because I had never done this before. I also did not want to fail Glenda by not making the team. Glenda had been a cheerleader for the past two years so she would have no problems making the squad. I was determined to make the squad and that is what I did. Glenda was selected as captain of the team that year. During our first practice, Glenda made an announcement that she needed to have a co-captain for the squad and that she had chosen me. I couldn't believe it. This was so much more than a title. It was more like a badge of honor.

After years of feeling unwanted and undeserving, I began to feel like I was somebody and that maybe I'd found a place to call home. However, in the back of my mind, there was still a monkey on my back. That monkey was still Mr. and Mrs. Brown. In time, I was able to see Mrs. Brown for the person that she was. She was not a real talker and never got overly happy or sad. She was not a person to freely hand out compliments. A person would have to earn them and not to expect to get them on a regular basis. Mr. Brown on the other hand seemed to be easy come easy go. In many ways, I found Mr. Brown easier to talk to than Mrs. Brown. However, my conversations with Mr. Brown were still a little weird and worrisome.

It was becoming more and more clear that my future at the Browns had potential. Yet, I was still cautious and on guard for bad things to happen. This fear came from the unknown of who Mr. and Mrs. Brown were. Why had they accepted me into their home? Was I simply a playmate for their daughter, or did they, or could they, accept me as myself? Do I really have a chance for being called "their daughter?" Only time would tell.

# Chapter 16
# Thorns in My Crown

The cold, dark wintery months were almost gone. Signs of spring would soon show their faces, as days become longer and the grass greener. This time of the year was a reminder that school would soon be over and plans for summer vacations would be next. I realized that the best vacation I ever had was going to Vacation Bible School. The Browns, being true born-again Catholics, would be clueless about Vacation Bible School. I suppose the only evidence I ever had to back up this claim was when I asked Glenda if she had ever been to Vacation Bible School It was pretty clear from her response that Vacation Bible School would not be of interest or excite the Browns. After having that conversation with Glenda, I decided it would be a waste of time to bring it up again. Just as I had thought this was a closed subject, Glenda surprisingly had more to say.

"Why in the world would anyone want to waste their summer going to church for summer vacation?" She also let it be known that anyone who did must be stupid and pretty lonely. I realized that day there would be more things from my past I would keep to myself.

I never again mentioned Vacation Bible School to anyone in that household. If my grandmother had been around to hear such hogwash, she would have washed Glenda's mouth out with a bar of lye soap. The summer months at the Browns' house were mostly about outdoor camping, bonfires, potlucks, and lots of mosquitos.

This kind of vacation wasn't exactly my cup of tea. I never understood how anyone got excited about sitting outside around a campfire, sweating, and eaten up by mosquitos. I never complained because I knew it would not change anything. A few of the camping trips did end with a silver lining, as I usually met a cute guy.

My grandmother had more old wise sayings than one could imagine and would often use them to teach us lessons about life and how to treat others. One of her favorite sayings was "nothing lasts forever." Fortunately, this was true about the boring camping trips. My first summer camping experience ended three weeks early, as Glenda and I had to start cheerleading practice for the upcoming football season. My first year as a cheerleader with the City League Park was better than I had ever expected it to be. Glenda deserved a lot of the credit for this because without her, I would have never been a cheerleader.

The season ended that year with our boys' football team losing in the regional championship tournament. Our team somehow got through the big loss. Our team didn't walk away empty, as they were recognized as 2$^{nd}$ runner up and received a trophy. The day of the championship game, Coach Jackson made an announcement that he had decided to honor both football players and cheerleaders by having a pizza party and a special awards ceremony at his home that evening.

The surprise announcement from Coach Jackson about the pizza party brought loud cheers, clapping, and the slinging off of jersey shirts into the air. Many of the cheerleaders reacted with their own excitement by strutting some of their best acrobatic moves before leaving the field. It was pretty clear we were all excited about the pizza party. You would never have known that we had just lost the championship game, as we were still proud of bringing home a trophy for taking 2$^{nd}$ place.

"O.K., you guys, we can celebrate more tonight. We got to get going," Coach Jackson continued. "There is another game starting on this field soon. So, go on now and get cleaned up for tonight."

Just as everyone started to scatter off the field, Coach Jackson yelled out another interruption. "Hey everyone, come back for just a minute! I need to mention one more thing before tonight's party. We will be voting tonight for a homecoming queen and king. So, put on your thinking caps and decide who you want to vote for. O.K. that's all. Go on home and get some rest and I'll see everyone later on tonight."

After Coach Jackson made that surprise announcement, I immediately turned to Glenda, but she was gone. Before I could give her another thought, I saw Billy Howell, the best-looking guy on the football team, headed in my direction. I panicked. My legs wanted to move, but they refused to cooperate. I found myself face to face with him.

"Are you coming to the party tonight?" he asked.

"Huh, I think so." I stammered a reply. "What about you?"

"Sure am!" He answered with a smile on his face.

"Well, I guess I'll see you tonight."

He wasn't finished. "Well, I wanted to also tell you something about tonight. I am going to vote for you for homecoming queen."

"Me? Why me?"

"Yeah, me and my buddies too. We want you to be homecoming queen."

"That's really nice of you. But are you really sure about this Billy? I mean don't you think that Glenda would make a good homecoming queen? I mean, she has been around a lot longer than I have. I guess what I am trying to say is, you need to be sure about all this Billy."

"Yep, I am really sure. See you tonight. Bye."

"Bye Billy. See you tonight."

Right after Billy ran off, I thought: *Wow, Billy Howell, the guy I've dreamed about all season long might like me.* But this business about me being homecoming queen, is so crazy and could be a big mistake. There's no way I'm going to get enough votes to become homecoming queen. I made up my mind that I would vote for Glenda and Mike Johnson. After convincing myself that Glenda would be crowned homecoming queen, I focused on finishing my homework and raiding my closet for something flashy to wear.

However, my thoughts drifted and selfishly, I thought about me and Billy becoming homecoming queen and king. These thoughts quickly vanished when I saw Glenda from a distance. She ran up and announced that she had found her missing pom poms. I was not particularly interested in her pom-poms. I wanted to know more about our plans for being able to go to the pizza party.

I quickly asked, "So, Glenda what about the pizza party tonight? Do you think we will be able to go?"

She spoke confidently, "Of course we will. I'm not missing this party. I might get voted as the City League's homecoming queen. Don't you think I have a good chance?"

"Yes, I do think you have a good chance. I'm voting for you."

Glenda changed the subject, "Hey, I just saw you talking to Billy Howell. I think he likes you."

"You do?"

Her answer seemed genuine, "I do. Billy doesn't talk to many girls. he was sure paying attention to you."

For some reason, I had a funny feeling about Glenda and me not being allowed to go to the pizza party because of having school the next day. I didn't want to miss out on the opportunity to spend time with Billy.

We were allowed to go to the party but had to do our homework before leaving. The only other glitch was Mrs. Brown drove us to the party and stayed the entire night. Glenda and I both agreed that she was probably up to something, especially because she heard the party wasn't going to be chaperoned. So, in the end, it was all about the boys and not trusting us. Hum, go figure.

The party was a big hit. Pizza and ice cream ran out after an hour, but no one seemed to care, as everyone continued to drink lemonade and dance. The music was loud and great for dancing. The best part of the night came when Billy Howell tapped me on the shoulder to ask if wanted to dance. He couldn't have asked me at a better time, as my favorite song, The Locomotion, started to play. The fun all started to end when Coach Jackson made the announcement that it was time for everyone to cast their vote for the homecoming queen and king.

Coach shouted out instructions for how we should cast our votes and then passed the football bowl around for everyone to place their folded paper in. Two parents, the head football coach and cheerleading coach counted the votes. I found it interesting that Mrs. Brown turned out to be one of those parents. The music was turned back up and a few people continued dancing until the votes had been counted. Billy was on the dance floor with a few other football players showing off his moves. There wasn't any real tension to speak of, as most of the cheerleaders had rallied around Glenda, who seemed to be anticipating being crowned homecoming queen.

Waiting for the results was more than I could handle. I began to feel sick to my stomach. I looked over to where Billy was standing, and he gave me two thumbs up and that's when I had to leave the room. I ran upstairs to the bathroom, to get myself together. *What was Billy up to?*

How long could I stay in the bathroom? I knew I had to go back downstairs and face the music. I had to go and support Glenda. I had to be around to congratulate her for winning the homecoming queen. Just as I approached the top of the steps that lead down to the basement, I overheard a loud shrill sound that came from a female shouting out, as if someone were having a disagreement or argument. The voice that I heard sounded angry. It was only seconds later that I realized that this voice belonged to Mrs. Brown.

I continued to linger around the top of the stairs. Well, it didn't take long to figure out the loud discussions and disagreements. It wasn't too long before I heard and figured out the disagreement and conflict behind closed doors. The bottom line was I received the most votes for being crowned as homecoming queen.

*How could something like this end up being an argument? You just simply add up the votes. What would be so hard about that?*

I became so distracted by what was going on with the votes that I didn't even care to get back to the others. This was probably a big mistake on my part. The next thing I heard was Mrs. Brown's voice above the others in the room. "This just can't be." Glenda should have won this crown."

A different loud female voice came back, "Well, she didn't win. The votes have been counted and Lauren is the official winner. We are not changing any votes in this room. That would be called cheating."

*Oh, my God, not me. I can't be the winner! I'm not the queen. The crown belongs to Glenda. What am I going to do?* Still in disbelief, I quickly rushed back down the stairs to join the others.

# Chapter 17
# Bittersweet Victory

The announcement finally arrived. The votes were in my favor. While I had just been honored as the new homecoming queen, I still struggled to enjoy the moment. How could I wear a crown that some said I didn't deserve or didn't win? Somehow, I managed to survive the final ceremonial festivities that included the awards banquet for both football players and cheerleaders. Shortly after this event, I packed away the crown and never mentioned it again. Things were never the same between me and Mrs. Brown. She was never to be trusted.

Over the next two months, things became less tense, as Glenda accepted my winning and moved on with her own life. However, I did receive an unexpected surprise that left me with hurt and disappointment. Without any explanation, Billy ended our relationship. There was something suspicious about this sudden breakup. It didn't take me long to solve this puzzle. It was a plot that Mrs. Brown could use against me for Billy's role in helping get me crowned as homecoming queen. Who knows what else that witch threatened Billy with.

I thought about Billy a lot that summer. However, these thoughts faded over time, but I became more focused and on guard with Mr. Brown. The summer that year seemed to have lasted a lifetime. I officially began high school that year and I was eager to start. I had even saved enough money to buy my own school clothes, as the days were over for depending on Mrs. Brown. One week before school started, Mrs. Brown announced during dinner that Mr. Brown would be renovating the bathroom that Glenda and I shared.

This was actually good news because this would mean that Glenda and I would get a new shower. Mr. Brown began the renovations right away and four days later, we had our new shower. Glenda and I were both excited because we had both bathed in a tub that was in a spare bedroom. The excitement led us to flip a coin to see who would get to shower first. I won the coin toss.

If the truth be known, Mr. Brown was a pretty darn good handy man around the house. However, on a sad note, most of his work and repairs were barely noticed and rarely received praise from Mrs. Brown. If anyone asked me, Mr. Brown did a bang-up job on the new bathroom. It reminded me of something you would see from a Sears & Roebuck catalog.

Honestly, I believe Mr. Brown worshipped the ground Mrs. Brown walked on and wanted her approval. But she, on the other hand, treated him pretty crummy. It was still hard for me to feel sorry for Mr. Brown because I knew he had the control and power to speak up for himself but decided to allow Mrs. Brown to dominate him. This was not my business, and anyway, my grandmother always told me, "You can lead a horse to water, but you can't make him drink." She also said, "once you've made your bed, you have to lie in it." If my grandmother could have spent a day or two with Mr. Brown, she would have been able to whip him into shape. If I'm honest, I felt sorry for Mr. Brown when Mrs. Brown told him to get lost.

But I can't let my guard down when I'm around him. He could take advantage or hurt me like so many had in the past. Since my break-up with Billy, Mr. Brown had been friendlier than normal and on occasion offered me a few extra dollars and asked if I needed a ride to the local drug store. I always politely turned down these offers and never regretted doing so. There were times when I should have perhaps accepted one of Mr. Brown's rides, as the path that gets you to the corner drug store isn't exactly the safest for a girl my age to take alone.

I guess I have been lucky, as I have walked this somewhat risky path a dozen times by myself without any real problems. The only time when I had a real scare was when a man on a motorcycle pulled up, stopped me in my tracks and asked me if I wanted to have sex. In reality, this man did not scare me, but he sure did insult me. I responded to this man, by telling him, "Real girls don't do that kind of dirty work." That was the end of that conversation. He sped off and I never saw him again. I also never walked that path again.

Summer was officially over, and the start of the new school year was only two days away. I was suddenly left with both sadness and happiness.

I thought about Billy and also the excitement of high school and new friends. I didn't want to focus on the past and decided that it was important to have a fresh start. I felt ready to start high school as a sophomore.

As I sat thinking all of this over in my mind, the idea of taking my first shower in the new bathroom felt just like the thing I needed. *Yeah, that's exactly what I need right now. Taking a hot shower would certainly relax me. Hum, let me find my favorite flannel robe to put on after I'm all nice and clean.*

Before I could reach for my purple flannel robe, there was a knock at my bedroom door.

"Hang on please." I was already half-way undressed and had to throw on my jeans and tee shirt before opening the door.

I opened the door and there stood Mr. Brown. Before I could say a word, he quickly blurted out, "I need you to do me a favor."

"O.K. What do you need me to do?"

"Well, there seems to be a little problem with the new shower. It's not draining quite right. But I think I may have it fixed. I need you to go and take a shower and that way we can see if the problem has been fixed."

"Sure, I was getting ready to take a shower anyway."

"Well, I need for you to do it right now."

"Yes sir, I will. Well, I do need to find Glenda first to ask her a question about it. So, it may be about 10 minutes before I can get in the shower."

"Glenda and her mother have gone out for a few minutes, so you can go on and get into the shower now."

"Oh, I never heard them leave. I'll get in the shower in about 5 minutes."

Mr. Brown made a quick exit and disappeared down the hallway. There was something about him and that conversation that just wasn't right. The more I thought about it, the more nervous and scared I became. I knew I had to think fast because he would be waiting. A plan suddenly popped into my head.

Suspecting he was up to no good, I knew what I would do. He must have thought I was just born yesterday. I tossed my flannel robe aside and quickly searched for my bathing suit. He will be in for the surprise of his life. He's not going to get the "hoochee-coochee" show that he thinks he is. *Hum, could I be over-thinking this? He has been awfully nice to me lately. But I just can't take a chance. One thing is for sure this man ain't seeing anything he shouldn't be seeing.*

Once fully dressed in my one-piece polka dot yellow and green swimsuit, I made my way into the shower. I must have been in the shower for about 5 minutes when I decided I would go ahead and wash my hair. As I reached up for the bottle of shampoo that was stored on a built-in shelf by the window, I spotted the image of a tall-like figure outside. I quickly pretended to ignore the image and continued with the shower. However, it was too late, this image then came in closer to the window and it was then that I saw the face of Mr. Brown.

I quickly finished my shower. As I tried to get myself together, my mind was flooded with thoughts of "How far will this man go? What am I going to do?" What I felt at that moment was sink or swim. It was clear that no one would be throwing me a life jacket. All I could settle on at the time was to stay afloat, keep my head above water, and be on high alert until I figured things out. What had become clear to me was neither of the Browns were to be trusted again.

# Chapter 18
# Heading for Trouble

My year as a high school sophomore was no walk in the park. The excitement and curiosity disappeared early that year, as I failed every single geometry test for the first semester. Math had never been a favorite subject of mine. My greatest fear that year was being unable to pass this class. The thought of being at the mercy of the Browns for their help created more fear and gloom. I would just have to cross that bridge when I needed to.

About half-way through the school year, I accepted my fate of being a failure, as I still had not passed one single geometry test all year. I had managed to delay the Browns from looking at my first semester report card. To be honest, it really wasn't that hard because they never asked to see my grades or how my classes were going. The bottom line, they were clueless.

As the semester went on, I kept on telling myself failing geometry wasn't a big deal. But it still nagged at me and felt important. I just didn't know what to do about failing this class. I did know one thing; I wasn't going to ask for any help from the Browns. It would be a cold day in hell before I did that.

There have been many times in my life when I was the only child without the support of a parent on school field trips or having the occasional surprise lunch visit from a parent. This has often left me alone to fend for myself. I decided that this situation would be no different. I would not panic, rather, I would postpone making any decisions until the end of fall break. Once I made peace with a plan, I was able to convince myself to relax and enjoy the next nine days of my fall break.

Well, things did not work out as planned. As I attempted to exit Mr. Thompson's geometry class, heading for the bus, I heard my name called out.

"Lauren, I need to see you for a moment." Mr. Thompson called to me.

"Yes sir?"

"I have something for you to take home to your parents. Please have them sign it, then bring it back after fall break. Now don't worry, you're not in trouble. I'm trying to find a way to help you with geometry."

"O.K. Thank you."

"Lauren, you are a hard worker. It shows in your homework assignments. I believe that for you, math may just be a difficult subject that might require some extra help."

"Thank you for giving me credit for trying."

"It's my job and I believe that you are good a student. I have seen your other grades. They are all "A's." Now you go and have a fun fall break."

I must have skipped all the way to the bus parking lot that day feeling hopeful about geometry. Also, Mr. Thompson provided me with encouragement, something that had been missing from my life. Once I had settled into my seat on the bus, I decided to open the letter that Mr. Thompson had written.

The letter was pretty much straight to the point. Mr. Thompson stated that I was a good student who was failing his geometry class. His last sentence was a request for the Browns to help me with my geometry. I had never expected Mr. Thompson to write this crazy part in the letter. How could he be so stupid? If only he knew the Browns.

The letter left me trapped with few options. The only two answers that came to me were that I could tear up the letter or pretend I never got it. *Why am I thinking about this crap? I should forget it for now. I'm on fall break. I'll think about this later. Hum, until then, I still need to find a place to hide it.*

Once I got off the bus, I made a decision to hide the letter in my bra until I made it home and was alone in my room. As a continued to walk home, I remembered a more positive event that had happened that morning during my first period English class. Mrs. Capps asked if I would be willing to tutor a student in English as a part of my final project. I wondered if she was thinking about hooking me up with one of those "boat people" who are from another country.

It really didn't matter who it was because I really felt honored and special that Mrs. Capps had asked me in the first place. If there was one thing my grandmother taught me, it was that all people should be treated the same. It didn't matter what color your skin was, how big or small your house was, the type of clothes you wore or how much money you carried in your pocket. Even though I didn't always agree with my grandmother on every one of these, I did agree on the skin color an individual had. Throughout my life, I have been treated and respected more by Black people than any other race.

As I approached the driveway of the Browns, it suddenly hit me that I had nine whole days without any school and could sleep in. But at the same time, I remembered that Mr. Brown had taken off a few days from work and would be around just enough to mess things up. I knew I would have to always be a few steps ahead of that man. Better yet, I would surprise all of them and be around as little as possible during the fall break.

I decided to make a list of things to do that would keep me busy and mostly out of Mr. Brown's reach. I had always loved books and the public library could be reached by bike. However, the bike ride was a challenge that sometimes could take about an hour and 45 minutes one way to get there. I had also decided to take my girlfriend, Patty, up on her offer to call her about going roller skating.

I temporarily felt a sense of relief in that I had a plan to survive for the next nine days being at home. Weekends at the Browns usually started with Friday night outings by going to Pizza Hut. We never got to choose the type of pizza we liked. Mr. and Mrs. Brown ordered and you either ate it or did without. I hated these trips because I usually got stuck next to Mr. Brown. I never understood why he and Mrs. Brown never sat next to each other.

Somehow, I managed to survive all nine days of my fall break and being around Mr. Brown. I also found the strength to peddle my way to the library on four occasions. I was disappointed that I missed hanging out with my friend Patty during my break, because her grandmother died, and she had to go out of town.

With only one day left of break before I had to return to school, Glenda asked if I would watch a WWF Wrestling TV show with her. She also told me, as if I had some knowledge of that kind of thing, that tonight's match featured her favorite wrestler, Rick Flair, who would be fighting for the world class championship. I had no idea what a wrestling match was about. I knew that my brothers had bickered and wrestled. So, I asked her if that was the same as her WWF wrestling. She answered me back with information about "cage fighting." I knew this was nothing like the wrestling that my brothers did.

Since the homecoming event, Glenda and I had not hung out together as much as before. I have always believed that her mother said or planted some kind of "bad seed" in her head about me. So, I felt that watching the wrestling show would be a way to get back on track with Glenda. I agreed to watch the show with her. At the dinner table that night, Glenda made it known to both Mr. and Mrs. Brown that she and I had first dibs on the TV, as we would be watching wrestling that night.

Mrs. Brown quickly barked orders that no TV shows would be watched until all homework assignments were collected.

"So, what time does the wrestling show start?"

Glenda replied, "Why are you asking Dad? Do you want to watch it with us? I thought you gave up watching wrestling. Anyway, I think it starts around eight o'clock. But the championship cage match with Rick Flare starts at nine."

*Oh, just great. Why can't he just find someone else to hang out with? Like maybe his wife?*

"Well girls, would it be okay. if I watch the match with y'all?"

"Sure, Dad" answered Glenda.

I never bothered to answer. I pretended that I was too busy to pay attention to his question, as I quickly cleared the dinner table. I was also scheduled to wash dishes for the night so the timing of that worked out well. I made a point in between washing the dishes to let Glenda know that I would meet her in front of the TV at eight sharp.

As I finished up the kitchen, I had a nagging feeling that I needed to do something for school, but nothing came to me. I thought to myself, it would come later on, particularly if it were important. Well, five minutes later it came to me. The letter from Mr. Thompson popped into mind. *Oh, no, what should I do?* Mr. Thompson would surely expect me to hand deliver this letter.

I just couldn't bring myself to do it. What excuse would I use? The only ones that came to me were the dog ate the letter, I lost the letter, the Browns refused to sign it, or the Browns just aren't interested in signing. I realized that none of these excuses were good or honest, except for maybe one of them. I decided at that moment I was not going to ask the Browns to sign the letter and that I would deal with Mr. Thompson somehow and in some way.

Glenda and I ended up watching most of the wrestling match alone that night. Mr. Brown joined us for the last 30 minutes. I never knew why he showed up late. He was surprisingly on his best behavior, as he minded his "P's" and "Q's" during the match.

Glenda was a happy camper that night as her favorite wrestler took home the brass buckle championship belt for heavy-belt WWF Championship Award. I had never seen such an animated side of Glenda, as she wanted to play out some of the wrestling moves that had been demonstrated by her favorite player, Rick Flair.

Glenda and Mr. Brown carried out some of these moves as they pretended to body slam one another and then pin one another in a head pin. I tried to be a good sport by cheering them on in victory. Things became a bit tense when Glenda summonsed me to rescue her by way of a tag-team move.

In a final attempt to play along, I innocently gave Glenda the tag only to become the opponent facing Mr. Brown. With no warning, Mr. Brown tackled me and placed his hands upon my breasts before he locked me in a body pin. The fun and my willingness to play along left me. I sprang forward and head-butted Mr. Brown, a move that I saw in the match, and freed myself.

It was pretty clear that Glenda did not see what went on when her father placed his nasty hands on my breasts. I believed this because she responded by cheering me on and seemed so content and happy, but it was no fun for me.

# Chapter 19
## It's Better to Give Than to Receive

I was probably the only kid in the world in the world who loved going back to school after having time off. School was an escape and a place where I found the freedom to be somebody and the courage to have an opinion.

Living at the Browns, I did not have either of these. What I experienced living at the Browns was just an "existence." I never received compliments or praise for anything. As much as I longed for approval and acceptance, I decided early on I was not going to beg or fall apart without their support. I considered myself lucky, because most of my teachers found something in me that made the difference in my success. Their support brought out the best in me and their attention made a difference in my life.

I survived fall break and couldn't wait to get back to school. I had so much to look forward to on my first day back. I had signed up to start working with my new math mentor and I was prepared to meet for the first time the student that I had been chosen to help tutor in English. Being excited with these two opportunities, I forgot all about the letter the Browns were supposed to sign. They didn't need to be involved.

The first day back to school ended great. Mr. Thompson was out sick, which gave me more time to deal with the "unsigned" letter and the dreaded Browns. At the same time, I knew that sooner or later Mr. Thompson would remember the letter and I would have to face the music. The only thing on my mind at the moment was to meet the student I would be tutoring. I would not spend time worrying about some ridiculous letter. It was shortly after lunch when Mrs. Capps introduced me to the student I was to tutor.

As I came face-to-face with the student, I panicked. I didn't know how to act or what to say. My grandmother would have said I had a case of "locked jaw." I must have looked pretty dumb and useless as I stood silent and couldn't speak the language that I was supposed to know so well. It was much later when it became clear to me why I froze up when I first met him. I had been caught off guard by his good looks.

Mrs. Capps saw exactly what happened. I had always been pretty good at thinking quick on my feet, but that day, it was like I had two left feet. Mrs. Capps rescued me by breaking the ice and introduced me to my student, Vu. There was very little that happened during that first tutoring session other than learning each other's name. In many ways, I was disappointed because I'd hoped to learn more details about how Vu escaped from Vietnam to the United States.

I left school that day still curious and excited as I thought about Vu and all the unknown things that I wanted to learn about him. The bus ride home that day ended too quickly. I dreaded going home. There were some days when I never knew who I would find there. Since Glenda and I began high school, Mrs. Brown started working as a substitute teacher, which often meant Mr. Brown would arrive home first. There were days when I got home from school and found Mr. Brown sitting around aimlessly staring at the wall and in my mind looking for trouble.

It didn't take many of those days before I figured a way to dodge coming home directly so I could avoid this good for nothing man. I found a back way to come home that allowed me to see what cars were parked in the driveway. On those days when I saw Mr. Brown's car, I stayed outside behind the storage shed that had a bench and small overhang that would protect me when it rained. I spent many days behind that shed alone with my thoughts, and also completed my homework. Spending this amount of time behind the storage shed was a way to stay out of the house until I needed to show up for dinner.

The first night at the dinner table, after the end of fall break, there was a conversation between Mr. and Mrs. Brown about a potential rendezvous after dinner. Mr. Brown started the conversation by blurting out to Mrs. Brown that he had taken an early bath and wanted to have some quiet and alone time with her. During dinner, Mr. Brown continued to tease and convince Mrs. Brown they should have some private time.

He continued emphasizing to Mrs. Brown that he had taken an early bath and asked if she wanted to smell him. Mrs. Brown quickly dismissed Mr. Brown's request and then changed the subject. It was no secret that Mrs. Brown had no desire to snuggle with Mr. Brown. She further reminded Mr. Brown that his "once a week" bath was not enough to excite or interest her.

After Mr. Brown was turned down twice, he finally accepted that he would not be getting what he desired for the night. After that night, it became clear that Mrs. Brown had little interest in romance with Mr. Brown. It also confirmed that Mr. Brown was a lonely man who was hungry for his wife. It also implied that Mrs. Brown is in charge and makes the rules.

Once Mr. and Mrs. Brown left dinner, Glenda and I cleared the table and washed the dishes. Glenda seemed sad and was not her usual chatty self. She was not interested in having any chit chat with me and rushed to her bedroom once the kitchen was cleaned. Before she made it to her bedroom, I managed to get her attention and began to share my exciting news about being asked to tutor a refugee student. I thought this might get her back to a happier place and distract her from being sad.

"Glenda, guess what I'm doing now at school?"

"I don't know. What?"

"I'm helping this Vietnamese guy learn how to speak English."

"You're doing what?" She seemed surprised.

"Mrs. Capps, the English teacher, asked me to help out with this project to tutor some of the students who came over on the boat from Vietnam.

"You mean, you're going to be helping a 'Chink'."

"What did you call him?" I was shocked and furious.

"A 'Chink'."

"He is not a 'Chink.' His name is Vu."

"What is his name?"

"You heard me, it's Vu. You spell it, V… U." I was working really hard to control my anger.

"Well, I'm not so sure that Mom will approve of you hanging around with a 'Chink'."

My voice gets much louder. "Stop calling him a 'chink.' I've told you his name twice."

Glenda continued, "Just remember that I warned you. Mom will not like it that you're hanging around someone who speaks a different language and who is that different. Now, there. I didn't call him a 'chink'."

"Well, it won't matter what your mom thinks. I've already made my decision to help him. He is a person just like we are. He is not a 'chink'."

I decided this conversation was over and walked away. Just as I approached the end of the hallway, I was stopped by Mrs. Brown.

The first thing that popped into my mind was I had to get past her and avoid any conversations. I got cold feet and blurted out the first thing that came to mind, "The dishes are done, and I have a lot of homework to get to, good night."

# Chapter 20
# Those Evil Eyes

I never spent any real alone time with Mrs. Brown. She wasn't exactly a person you'd choose as a roommate or bunk with during a summer camp vacation. I had already decided that in the future, if I got married and had children, I would not want my children to call her grandmother. I even questioned if I would want her and Mr. Brown at my wedding? While Mr. Brown seemed to be the one I struggled to create the most distance from, it seemed that later on Mrs. Brown made it to the top of this list.

Mrs. Brown reminded me of a stalker who had eyes in the back of her head. She would strike when you least expected. My first experience with this side of her happened one night when she cornered me at the end of the hallway after dinner. Mrs. Brown had surely plotted this event, as she never wasted her time on me. Being face to face with Mrs. Brown, I was forced to stare at her dark, deep-set eyes that were sunken into the rest of her monstrous face.

I realized there was nowhere to go. But what did this stalker want from me? What were these eyes saying to me? The awkwardness and tension slowly screamed out, but nothing was spoken. Then Mrs. Brown reached into her pocket and pulled out a piece of paper. What could that be? Maybe she is giving me my walking papers. Thank God; that would be great.

She finally began speaking, "I found something that belongs to you. It was under the picnic table outback. You must have dropped it this afternoon."

Just as I was about to tell her thank you, she interrupted me with a sharp comment. "I did open it because I didn't know what it was. I didn't know you were having trouble in your math class. Do I need to sign this letter?"

"Yes Ma'am. I'm not very good at math. I do have someone who is helping me at school now."

"O.K. Now, don't keep things like this from us. We could get in trouble if we don't know about these things."

"What do you mean about you getting in trouble? It's my responsibility to learn the math."

She came back hard, "I know what I'm talking about. I just need to sign all forms that come home."

"Is that all you need to talk about?" I was afraid that she would bring up Vu.

After a period of uncomfortable silence, "There's nothing else tonight, that's all for now."

"O.K. I will make sure that I bring all forms home right away. Good night."

I was waiting to hear a good night from Mrs. Brown before I turned away to my bedroom, but it turned into another awkward moment, as her eyes pierced into mine and wouldn't let go. Fortunately, I was saved by footsteps echoing down the hall, announcing that someone was about to join us.

Mrs. Brown finally added a curt "Goodnight."

I rushed into my room and flopped face down on the bed. I had to get that image of her face erased from my memory. My grandmother used to talk a lot about evil acts of the devil. I started to believe that Mrs. Brown could be related to the devil, as her eyes were filled with mystery, anguish, and coldness. I reassured and calmed myself when I remembered something else that my grandmother taught me, "good things in life do happen for those who are patient and who believe."

What a good way to end the night, by going to sleep feeling close in mind and spirit with my late grandmother. Just as I had committed to this, I saw the crumpled-up letter that was to be returned to school, unsigned. How could she not have signed it? After all that drama, she did not sign it? Wow! O.K. I will fix that. I will just go and knock on her door and have her sign it. She made such a big fuss over this unsigned letter, now it was my turn.

I knew that my decision to knock on her door at 10:00 at night would not be a good idea, but I didn't care. However, one thought did occur before I left my room. What if I interrupted Mr. and Mrs. Brown having sex? I knew that the chances of that happening would be a cold day in hell. If this happened, they would just have to deal with it.

Just as I opened my door to walk into the hallway, I caught a glimpse of Glenda walking into Mrs. Brown's bedroom. I immediately wondered what they were up to. I suddenly had a funny feeling about all of this. Were they conspiring about my tutoring the so called "chink," aka Vu? Perhaps I was blowing this all out of sorts?

A part of me wanted to rush inside Mrs. Brown's bedroom and demand she sign my letter. Yet another side told me to wait until tomorrow. Before I was able to make a decision, I heard Mrs. Brown's door open and loud sobbing. Then right in front of me darted Glenda, who raced down the hallway towards her bedroom.

I had no idea what just happened between them. I suppose Mrs. Brown is capable of evil acts even to her own daughter. Hopefully, Glenda will mention something to me tomorrow about what happened between the two of them.

I tossed and turned most of that night, wondering if Glenda told Mrs. Brown about Vu. I had never seen Glenda so upset. The next morning, Glenda was a no-show at breakfast. This was not a good sign. Glenda never missed a meal. I pretended to not have much of an appetite that morning and left breakfast early. I was eager to get to the bus stop to find Glenda.

Once I made it to the bus stop, I found Glenda with her head buried in a book and not interested in talking to anyone. Finding her in that state, I decided it was best to give her time and space. I decided to distract myself by also reading a book that was three weeks past due.

Before I had a chance to read a sentence, Glenda blurted out, "I hate my stupid mother."

I quickly tossed my book aside and replied, "What did you say?"

"I said I hate her."

"You hate Mrs. Brown, your mother?"

"Yes, I do."

"Did something happen between y'all?"

There was a moment of awkward silence then Glenda went on, "She just doesn't understand. It's always her way. I will show her."

"Gosh, this all sounds pretty serious. Are you sure you're alright?"

"Yep, I'm going to be, once I go to the Health Department after school today."

"What? Are you sick?"

"Nope."

"I'm sorry, this is all confusing. It's not any of my business but I am worried about you." I felt I was being a little nosey, but I really did want to help.

"No, it's O.K. I need to tell you. I am getting me some birth control pills."

"Why?"

"Because I am having sex."

# Chapter 21
## You Can't Judge a Book by Its Cover

During the last two months of my freshman year in high school, I began to look at situations and people in different ways. I had also realized that I needed more than "book-smarts" to make it the world. It was more about having common sense that would make the difference in a person's life. My grandmother had always believed that a person could not buy common sense and that not everyone would be lucky enough to have such a thing.

It was at the end of my freshman year that I realized no one in the Brown household had any common sense. Rather, I saw them as the "blind leading the blind." This had particularly been the case as Mrs. Brown described Glenda as a "holy child" and believed that she could do no wrong. I, on the other hand, had been described as a "poor lost soul" who had been fortunate to be given a second opportunity to make something out of myself.

While I never outwardly voiced my true feelings and resentment to Mrs. Brown, I knew the truth. I was not a lost soul trying to find myself.

I managed to pull up my grades during that freshman year, as I averaged five A's and believe it or not, I squeezed out a B minus in my Geometry class. I continued to tutor Vu twice a week; we even started having lunch together on Fridays. The tutoring lessons quickly developed into more of a close friendship. He became more and more fluent in English which allowed for us to laugh and understand each other better.

As I continued my tutoring sessions with Vu and picked up odd jobs around the neighborhood: babysitting, cutting grass and washing cars, Glenda and I saw less and less of each other. However, this is also when I came to know a very different Glenda. The Glenda that I once knew as this so called, "goody-two-shoes" girl had changed into a completely different person.

Those conversations that once centered on WWW wrestling matches and cheerleading practices switched to secretive talks as Glenda insisted that she share graphic details of her sexual activities with her boyfriend. I often struggled to change the topic of those uncomfortable and embarrassing conversations but was never successful. She endlessly bragged about a new sex position or how much fun I was missing. These conversations with Glenda eventually became less and less frequent, as she lost interest in me and spent most of her time with her boyfriend.

Glenda became known as one of those "fast girls" among friends at school; this also created further distance and tension between us. I made up my mind that I had to be a separate person from Glenda and would have no connection with her during my time at school. I was successful in using this approach until I fell into a "Glenda trap."

Glenda stopped riding the school bus, as her boyfriend had a car and drove her back and forth to school. This had been a miracle because I had been able to ride the bus and make new friends without that connection with "fast Glenda." The last day of school during my freshman year ended with the usual bus ride home. However, this bus ride home included an unexpected passenger, Glenda.

I had taken my usual seat located eight rows behind the bus driver. Everyone already on the bus had made their way into conversations with friends about their plans for the summer; some voiced complaints about demands for having to go to summer school. I was involved in a conversation with a friend who invited me to join her for a few days at her church summer camp. I never expected an invitation from this particular girl, as everyone wanted to be liked by her. I was excited and honored at the same time that she invited me and wanted to quickly accept her offer. Just as I attempted to give my acceptance of her offer, I saw Glenda walking down the bus aisle.

What was she doing riding the darn school bus? I didn't need her here to mess up my plans with my friends. Maybe I can ignore her. I took note that there were no seats near me, so she probably won't even come back this way. But it was too late. Before I knew it, there she stood right in front of me. My God, what was wrong with her? Her neck was broken out in a red rash.

Awkwardly and loudly, I blurted out, "Glenda what are you doing on this bus?

"Well, let's see, I guess you could say, I am riding it. Just like everyone else."

It was clear that she was upset. She hadn't ever been smart to me in the past. I wondered what was wrong with her neck. Should I ask her? Would it embarrass her?

Just as I was about to ask her if she was OK, another person on the bus shouted out, "Gross, what's that crap on your neck? Don't sit next to me? I don't want that shit on me?"

Another person chimes in, "Dang, don't you get something like that sleeping around?"

I couldn't believe what I was hearing. Why hasn't Glenda said anything?

It didn't take very long before Glenda finally fired back. "It ain't no big deal. I guess y'all haven't ever heard of "hickeys" have you?" Several kids shouted back, "Whatever it is, looks pretty nasty and I don't want any of it."

It was at that time, one girl stood up and said, "I know what those thangs are, my mom gets those from her boyfriends. They are nasty."

The bus driver approached the back of the bus and demanded to know what the noise was all about. The problem was solved by the driver taking Glenda to the front, away from the teasing comments of the other students. But for me, the conversation with my friend was history and the chances for an invitation was ruined. Glenda and I soon got off the bus together and walked the short distance home without speaking. I wondered how Mrs. Brown would handle this? I never found out. Glenda and I grew further apart, with almost no interactions and certainly no friendship.

# Chapter 22
# A Surprise Summer

The end of another school year passed, and I was probably the only girl who felt little excitement about having a summer vacation. There were no vacations or summer camps to look forward to. I suppose the best part of summer would be not waking up to an alarm clock every morning and looking forward to tutoring Vu a couple days a week.

After just two weeks of summer vacation, I woke up to find Mr. Brown home from work. The first thought that came to mind was I must be dreaming. My gut inclination that day was to camp out in my room for most of the day. I was able to sneak out of my room to grab a snack and return without running into him.

Later on in the afternoon, I heard Glenda ask her dad why he was home on a Friday. His reply back to Glenda was he had decided to take off on Fridays for the summer. I couldn't believe it. I wanted to scream out, "No, you can't." Once this news had sunk in, it didn't take long for me to come up with a plan to work around this crap. I would switch one of the days for tutoring Vu to Friday. I would also continue to search for a part-time job.

I had never discussed any of my summer plans with Mrs. Brown. I had pretty much convinced myself that she wasn't interested in my life. There had been a few times when it had crossed my mind that perhaps I should have written her a letter about my summer plans. The trip to the library was five miles and the possibility of something happening to me, like getting hit by a car, was a risk. The bottom line was that Mrs. Brown was responsible for me whether I liked it or not. The bike ride was an activity that I looked forward to. That particular summer, I saw very little of Mrs. Brown, as she was involved in an organization called the "Eastern Star." I never learned or knew what she actually did with this group. I often overheard her talk to Mr. Brown about her involvement in activities in the community with the Eastern Star.

The more time that Mrs. Brown spent away from the house, it became even more important to pay closer attention to Mr. Brown's schedule, in an attempt to avoid being around him. Glenda rarely came around during the summer other than an occasional unannounced drive-by visit to pick up clean clothes and to exchange old cassette tapes for different ones. Clearly, our lives had started to go down different paths.

My weekly tutoring sessions with Vu provided an outlet and gave me purpose. It was always a relief and a joy to spend time with him, as I knew I was doing a good thing. After about eight weeks of tutoring, Vu had mastered some of the basic English language skills that gave him confidence to talk with friends and his teachers. On one particular day at the library, Vu unexpectedly handed me a worksheet assignment that we agreed he would complete towards the end of the summer. This final assignment would serve as a guide to measure his progress and help determine if he needed to continue with a tutor in his sophomore year.

I found it a little unusual that Vu gave me his final assignment two weeks early. I decided not to make a big deal out of it and to accept it. The assignment was given to me in a sealed envelope. This also caught my attention, but I decided not to ask any questions. At the end of our tutoring session, Vu asked if I would correct the paper and bring it back for next week's tutoring session. My curiosity continued to grow, but I once again agreed to Vu's request, and we said our good-byes until next week's session.

Following that tutoring session, I lingered around the library and decided to do some research on the organization called "Eastern Star." My curiosity had gotten the best of me regarding Mrs. Brown and her being a member of this club. I continued to have a hard time believing that she served others when she was not able to show any kindness in her own home. I found the information that I needed, and it did not match the Mrs. Brown that I knew. I left the library that day with an even deeper feeling of disrespect for this woman.

As I rode my bike home that day, I made peace with myself that Mrs. Brown was someone that I would never really like. However, I also realized that I didn't have to hate her. My own common sense, and what I learned from my grandmother, told me that such feelings are the work of the devil. I had also known and been taught that hating others would not get you into heaven. In the past, my grandmother would not have thought twice before reminding me of the Ten Commandments when I threatened my younger brothers, with outbursts of "I hate you."

My first big surprise that summer took place when I opened the envelope that contained Vu's completed homework assignment. Inside the envelope, I found what looked like a letter that was addressed to me. At first glance, I was confused by the letter as I continued to search for the missing homework. Once I realized there was no homework in the envelope, I decided it made sense to open the letter.

Once I had the letter opened, I must have read it 10 times or more.

*"Dear Lauren,*

*I like you very much a lot. Would you like me a lot?*

*I want to be your boyfriend. Will you be my girlfriend too?*

*Yes, or no?"*

I felt that Vu deserved an answer to his letter, particularly after he worked so hard putting together almost complete sentences. My answer to him was a big check mark "Yes." Vu and I secretively "went together" the rest of that summer. We pretty much got to see each other twice a week when I tutored him at the library and on occasion when we talked on the telephone. Even though we were officially going together, it really didn't feel much different than being close friends. Vu was gentle, kind and never once tried to take advantage of me. There had been a time or two I had wished he had been maybe just a little naughtier.

Just when summer had begun to wind down, I received one more surprise from Vu that left me feeling happy but confused. Vu surprised me at our last tutoring session by sharing that he passed his driver's license exam. I had no idea he was working towards getting his license. He also asked if he could drive me back and forth to school. You would have thought he had won a million dollars. He seemed so happy and proud that he was able to make me this offer.

Before I was able to answer him, I redirected the conversation by asking to see his driver's license picture. I had such feelings of guilt as I had not told the Browns about Vu and me going together. I'm not sure why I had kept it from them. It was at that moment, I decided it was time to tell them. I made a deal with myself to tell them later that night.

Finally, I responded to his question, "Wow, look at you. That's a great picture. You look so cute."

"You like my picture? I don't look funny?"

"No. You look smart."
"Well, can I drive you to school?
"Yes, I think it would be great for you to pick me up."

# Chapter 23
# Growing Up

I managed to survive another boring summer at the Browns. I suppose what helped me was the time I spent with Vu and those long bike rides back and forth to the library. Those trips kept me away from home and away from Mr. Brown.

The excitement of Vu getting his license that summer didn't turn out the way he planned. Two weeks after he began driving the car his father gave him, the engine blew. I later learned that Vu forgotten to add oil to the car. Being without a car really sucked for a lot of reasons. First it meant a delay in Vu meeting the Browns. Also, the loss of the car would mean less time with Vu and more time at home.

Vu and I had also made plans to spend the day together for my 16th birthday. However, we both had to make peace with the fact this wasn't going to happen without a car. It didn't stop us from brainstorming other ways for us to be together. Vu tried to borrow his dad's car on the day of my birthday, but somehow that didn't work out. I ultimately accepted the fact that I would be celebrating another lonely birthday with people not of my choice. This became even more hopeless when I learned I had to wake up at 5:30 a.m. to go pick strawberries in 95-degree weather.

*How could anyone with any brains make someone pick strawberries, in scorching heat, on their birthday? Maybe I would eat so many strawberries that I would get sick and have to come home early.*

Fortunately, I was rescued that day by a nasty thunderstorm that forced all pickers to leave the field. In many ways, I considered that storm a birthday gift and left the strawberry patch with a smile on my face. During the drive back home, Glenda and I were reminded that we would be back to visit the strawberry patch at a later date. I heard very little of anything else Mrs. Brown said the rest of the way home, as I couldn't wait to get home to talk to Vu.

As Mrs. Brown made the final turn onto our street, I realized that Mr. Brown would not be home from his job and quickly changed my plans. I decided to put off my call to Vu and to take my bath while Mr. Brown was away. *Maybe my birthday will take a turn around now that we've left that stupid strawberry patch.*

It was at this moment, I heard Mrs. Brown blurt out, "Who is that Black boy up there snooping on our porch? I bet he's looking for a house to break into. Well, it sure want be my house."

Glenda who had dozed off, jumped up from the back seat and blurted out, "What's all the fuss about? Is something wrong, Mom?"

It was about that time the car had made it close enough to the house where I could see who was standing on our porch. Without any warning, I cried out, "That person isn't trying to break into our house. I know him. That's my boyfriend, Vu."

Before I could get out another word, Mrs. Brown commandingly asked, "Who did you say that boy was?"

'That is Vu. He is my boyfriend. I'm sure he came to surprise me today for my birthday. I've been wanting you to meet him."

"Is he a *Black* boyfriend?"

Before I was able to answer Mrs. Brown, Glenda joined the conversation. "No mom, don't you remember that night after dinner, we were all talking about Vu and him being a 'Chink'."

I knew at that moment I was about to explode and needed to say something. "Okay, both of you, stop it, that's enough. How dang rude. If I've told y'all once, I'll tell you again, Vu is not a 'Chink.' He happens to have a nationality, and it is Vietnamese. How would y'all like to be called, 'rednecks or white trailer trash?' It wouldn't be any different. Stop calling my boyfriend names that just aren't true."

I was surprised that Mrs. Brown allowed me to speak out so boldly and chose not to answer back with some kind of remark. All of a sudden, the silence turned to uncertainty, as I wondered what Mrs. Brown was thinking. After what seemed like an eternity, Mrs. Brown finally had something to say.

"So be it. Since today is your birthday, I'm going to let this slide. Let's just get this meeting thing over with. I'm not looking my best after sweating and being out in the sun, to meet anyone."

*Get this thing over? She makes me sick. I can't wait until the day I leave this hell hole.*

Once we pulled into the driveway, Vu made his way down off the porch toward the car. I noticed two wrapped gifts in his hand. Before I knew it everyone was face to face and there was silence. Who would break the ice? Of course, it should be me.

"Vu, thanks for coming today. How did you get here? Did your dad drop you off?" For a few seconds, Mrs. Brown was erased from my day.

Without really thinking, I realized that I should have first introduced him to Mrs. Brown. Before I could give any more thought to that, I heard Vu's voice.

"Happy Birthday, Lauren." I rode my bike here today. My Dad couldn't bring me. I have something to give you for your birthday today. Oh, I also have something for your mom."

I couldn't believe it, how perfect was that? My boyfriend surprised me on my birthday, and he tried to get brownie points with Mrs. Brown.

"You brought us gifts? Wow, that is so exciting. Well, I really want to introduce you to Mrs. Brown, because she has been waiting to meet you." I had no idea why I said that.

Before Mrs. Brown had any opportunity to utter a word, Vu started the conversation.

"Hi Mrs. Brown, I'm Vu. I like Lauren much. She is nice to me. I can talk English a lot better now because she has helped me. My English is still not very good, but it will get better real soon. Look, I bring you a gift today. I hope you will like it."

*Why did he bring her a gift? Was he crazy? Of course, he would bring her something, it was the right thing to do. The question was would she accept it and thank him? Or rather show her ass and embarrass me? Wait a minute, I should be getting a gift, it's my birthday, not hers.*

Mrs. Brown surprised me by accepting the gift and jokingly commented, "What did I do to deserve such a gift?"

It took everything within my being not to blurt out, "not a damn thing." But that would have been so unfair to Vu and clearly would not support my relationship with Vu.

It was clear that Vu had no idea what Mrs. Brown had asked. Vu smiled and continued to repeat, "You like it?"

Mrs. Brown announced that she would delay opening Vu's gift until after dinner and would talk to him later about it. Vu seemed to OK with what she said. I had hoped that Vu would have been invited to dinner that evening, however that did not happen. I still invited Vu to stick around for a snack before he made his 20-mile bike ride back home.

We sat out on the front porch away from everyone and had a chance to talk and get in a few laughs. I managed to keep track of the time, as it was important that Vu be gone before Mrs. Brown started yelling out her dinner commands.

Running out of new things to talk about, our conversation eventually slowed down. It had turned out to be a great day from picking strawberries getting rained out to ending the day with a surprise visit from Vu. It was the best present I could have asked for. The visit ended as Vu thanked me for the snacks and asked if he could come again soon. Before I was able to answer, he reached into his pocket and handed me a small gift.

"Oh, I forgot, I have you something for your birthday. Sorry I didn't give it to you before. I know you might like it."

"Can I open it before you leave?"

"Yes, you can. You don't have to wait like your mom…I mean Mrs. Brown." We both laughed out loud.

I opened the box slowly yet eagerly wanting to know what it was. Finally, I had the box opened and found a beautiful green jade bracelet. I wasn't able to say anything. I was speechless. Why did he give me such a beautiful and seemingly valuable gift?

It was minutes before I could speak. "Wow, I love this. I don't believe that you gave me this. It is so special and pretty."

This bracelet was my mother's. I want you to wear it."

Once again, I had no words. I felt honored and loved.

"Will you wear it?"

"Yes, I will wear it."

I wanted to say so much more to Vu. However, I knew that he needed to be on his way. We both said our good-byes and managed to sneak in a hug. I had longed for him to stay longer that night. However, I knew at the same time, we had made progress and would continue to move forward. After Vu left, I cleaned up for dinner and prepared myself for lots of questions from Mrs. Brown.

Dinner ended up being a birthday surprise, as Mrs. Brown and Glenda took me out for pizza. Mr. Brown worked late and did not join us, which I considered a birthday gift. Conversation that night at the Pizza Hut was dominated by Glenda, as she had been trying for weeks to con Mrs. Brown into allowing her to go to the beach for a weekend trip with her boyfriend. Sensing her mom had not been convinced that Glenda had all the facts surrounding this trip, she quickly changed the conversation. Without hesitation, I blurted out, "So, what do y'all think about Vu?"

Glenda spoke first. "He seems o.k. to me. I think he's into you. I mean anyone that will ride a bike 20 miles to see a person must care about them."

I chose not to respond because Mrs. Brown needed to say something. Anything. Just something. I made a quick glance her way and she seemed far away, somewhere in deep thought. The next thing I heard was Glenda's voice.

"Mom, you must have something to say about him. I mean, he did bring you a gift."

"Yes, he seems like an O.K. boy. If you like him that's all that matters."

I couldn't believe that was all she had to offer. I felt like throwing up all three slices of pizza right in her face. Instead, I said. "Well, he is O.K. But he's really much more than O.K. He is great. I am the luckiest girl in the world because of him."

It was a quiet ride back home that night other than the radio playing. I wondered what Mrs. Brown would do with the gift that Vu gave her. I realized that I forgot to ask him what the gift was. I would find out tomorrow when I talked to him. I didn't have to wait to ask Vu about the gift, as Glenda then asked Mrs. Brown if she had decided where to hang the "Jesus" picture.

Mrs. Brown either ignored Glenda or she failed to hear the question. Glenda repeated the question only this time she lightly tapped her mother on her shoulder hoping to get her attention and an answer.

"No, I haven't. I don't know when I will have or find the time to either. When I do, I'll let you know."

# Chapter 24
## I'm in the Driver's Seat

It remained a mystery as to what Mrs. Brown ended up doing with the portrait that Vu had given her. I had decided that she wasn't worth my time and energy. My mind was made up, I would not beg for any of her attention. Vu eventually stopped asking about Mrs. Brown's approval of the portrait, after I decided to lie and tell him that Mrs. Brown had found a special place for the portrait. Lying is something that I was never good at or proud of. Vu seemed satisfied with my answer and moved on.

The truth was, I knew that someday I would confess the truth to Vu, and he would understand. I also made peace with myself on that day, as I remembered what my grandmother told me about telling the truth and a lie. She said, "the good Lord, knows a person's true heart and is a forgiving Lord." I had hoped that the Lord would look down on my soul and know that my true heart did not belong to a sinner.

I continued to have a hard time looking Mrs. Brown in the eye, as I knew she was never to be trusted as long as I lived under her roof. The timing of the start of a new school year had once again been a familiar solution to my survival at the Browns. My junior year became the year I hungered for success and for a life beyond the Browns.

In a strange way, life became more manageable at the Browns. I saw less and less of everyone. It seemed that we all had our own agenda and went about our days ignoring each other. The family dinners even changed. Sunday became the only definite time we gathered around the table to eat. I never went hungry, and food was never rationed or withheld as it had been in previous foster homes.

In many ways, my junior year of high school prepared me for a life beyond the confines of living with the Browns. I was involved in multiple school clubs, participated on the gymnastic team and was the assistant editor-in-chief for the school newspaper. I also found myself surrounded by the more popular kids at school and was highly respected by my teachers. On many days, I had to remind myself where I really came from and to not lose sight of my roots in the excitement of popularity and achievement.

There were days I had to slow down the momentum and think about my boyfriend, Vu. He had become a special person in my life. In spite of increased activities during my junior year, I continued to spend more and more time with Vu. He had managed to piece together a car during that summer and picked me up every morning for school. We had become an "item" among our peers and even to some of the teachers. We were no longer known as the "tutor and the student."

There also came a time when Vu made it known that I was more than just a "girlfriend." Time quickly slipped into early November and many of us turned our attention to talking about the holidays. Vu reminded me during that early November that he needed to get a part-time job during the holidays so that he could buy me a special gift. It was only three days later when I received a telephone call from Vu with exciting news; he had been offered a part-time job pumping gas at a Sunoco Gas Station.

His job was a good thing as it allowed Vu to help his father out. He developed a great relationship with his boss and in a short period of time proved himself a responsible and honest worker. There had been a few occasions when Vu called into work late as a result of driving me home from school. I decided that Vu had worked too hard to find a job to risk losing it over me and decided to do something about it. After I had confirmed the amount of money I had in my savings account, I informed the Browns I was ready to buy a car of my own.

Surprisingly, Mrs. Brown shared that her brother had a car business and suggested that I look at a few cars in his car lot. She also reminded me that buying a car from her brother would be much cheaper than going to a private car dealer. Mr. Brown felt the need to assure me that he would inspect the car before I purchased it. There was something about this deal that seemed "too good to be true." I was certainly okay about saving money, but I could not trust Mr. Brown. The day we were scheduled to go look at cars began on a negative note. I received a knock on my door early on a Saturday and was greeted by a smiling Mr. Brown, informing me that he would be taking me to go look at cars. He eagerly told me that Mrs. Brown wasn't feeling well. The first thought that flashed through my mind was "I'd rather walk in hail, thunder and lightning before I ride alone in a car with you buddy."

I pretty much knew my options were limited that day. It was either take the risk with Mr. Brown or risk missing out on an affordable car. I decided to take a chance. However, I would be on guard for any of his nonsense. The trip ended up being an all-day event, as Mr. Brown had received bad directions to the car lot.

Once we finally found the car lot, no one was there. We found a cardboard sign, hanging from a tree that read, "We are feeling hungry. Back soon." Just my dang luck. Here I am out in the boondocks with this crazy man for who knows how long. Before I was able to think any further, the lunch junkies drove up. Mr. Brown left me in the car and went to talk with Mrs. Brown's brother.

It was a relief to have a moment to myself and was able to get a sneak preview of some of the cars. It didn't take long to see the only two rusty cars on the lot. Mr. Brown made his way back to me and announced, "So, are you ready to start looking at the cars?"

"What cars? I mean, I've already seen those two beat-up rusty cars over there."

"Now, don't get ahead of yourself. I'm going to check out these cars for you. Don't you remember what I promised you?" All I could think of was this could be a mistake. However, I knew I needed to get this over. Somehow, I managed to pick between one of the two rusty cars and paid my $500. At the same time, I was haunted by thoughts of "how would I be able to drive this car to school?"

I would clearly have to park the car at least a mile away from school and others. This car could be the end of my popularity and hard-earned image among my friends and teachers. Mr. Brown appeared much more enthusiastic about this car adventure than I was. My lack of interest led to me being distracted by a stray dog that had suddenly appeared from behind the garage.

"Ha. Did you come here to look at cars or dogs? Come on over here now and make sure you've made the right choice." It would have been a much better day if I had shown up to get a cute dog rather than one of those rusty, stinking, greasy old cars.

"I've made up my mind already. I will take the old beat-up white one. There were several special things about this car over the other car. This car had windshield wipers and a horn that worked. One of the not so special things about this car was the floor had small holes which reminded me of a "Fred Flintstone" car.

Before I was allowed to seal the deal, Mr. Brown insisted that I take the car out for a test drive. It really made no sense to take this car out for a test drive. In the end, I agreed because in my mind it would be a step closer to getting me away from Mr. Brown and back home.

Once I found myself settled into the rusty old white Chevelle, I followed a mental checklist from my summer Drivers Ed Program, as I adjusted all the mirrors, positioned my seat, and slowly started the ignition. Before I knew it, I had the car traveling down a two-lane road. For a few brief moments, I completely forgot about Mr. Brown being anywhere in sight.

However, this all changed when I realized I didn't know where I was going. Also, I wasn't sure of the speed limit. I had made my mind up that I would not be talking to Mr. Brown during the test drive, but I realized I needed someone to navigate where I would be driving and how to get back to the car lot.

Also, I needed some help with finding out what the speed limit was. The last thing I needed would be getting stranded out in the middle of nowhere and get a speeding ticket. But all of these problems took care of themselves as Mr. Brown blurted out. "Now watch your speed, there's a tricky curve up yonder around the bend. I know this area a lot better than you do. This ain't no race here, so slow down. You need to be taking your time and enjoying this little ride."

"Look, this ain't no joy ride, just tell me what the dang speed limit is."

"Now, you don't have to be so snappy here."

I chose not to answer back with any comments or apologies and continued to drive slowly and cautiously. Finally, I was greeted by a road sign that had the speed limit posted. Shortly after I had passed the speed limit sign, I saw a turnaround spot that would make for an opportunity to head back to civilization. This decision brought about some tension between me and Mr. Brown, as he tried to convince me that I needed to drive the car a little further.

"What are you doing girl?"

"Are you talking to me?"

"You need to drive this car a little further. It has been siting for a long time on the car lot."

I continued to drive but it wasn't in the direction of Mr. Brown's liking. I stayed focused on driving and did not offer any more chit chat. While at the same time, I braced myself for his next words or actions.

"Well, ain't you happy about this car? You haven't acted happy all day. You act like you are mad or scared. Did one of those men back at the car lot say something to you? You know you can tell me if they did."

Before I was able to get any words out of my mouth, I felt something pressing onto the upper part of my leg. For a brief moment, I wanted to believe that my purse had fallen over into my lap but then a sick feeling came over me. I knew what that touch was all about and who touched me.

Mr. Brown had located a spot between my legs where he wanted to rest his nasty hand. Amazingly, I somehow managed not to wreck the car while knocking his nasty hand off my leg. Once I regained my thoughts, I found myself caught behind a damn old timer in a no-passing zone.

Once the slow driver turned off the road, I shouted out "Keep your nasty old grungy hands off my body. You are just a dirty old man who tries to hurt others. Just like that day when you tried to trick me into taking a shower in the new bathroom so you could see me naked. What's wrong with you? Did you have a bad childhood like me? Well guess what, get some help or get over it. I am not your play toy."

"We don't need to talk about my childhood. Now, I have no plans to hurt you. You should know better than that. Why would I give up my Saturday and drive you to the country to buy a car if I wanted to hurt you? Now do you want to buy this car or not? You need to decide before we get back there."

I had nothing else to say to him. I would discuss my plans for buying the car with Mrs. Brown's brother. The thought of driving this monster of a car to school was frightening. I would surely be banned from the school parking lot. Once we returned, I made my way into the garage to find George to finalize the deal. It felt as if I had handed over all my life's possessions. I worked long and hot summer days to earn that amount of money. It was the most money I had ever held in my hand. At the same time, it was a good feeling that at the age of 16, I was able to buy my own car with the money that I earned.

"So, how did you like ole Bessie?'

"Yes sir, the car will do just fine. It will get me to the places that I need to go to. Thank you for your help." As I completed the car deal, it was a relief to not have Mr. Brown breathing down my back. This was the best move and decision he made all day. As I started to walk away from George, he shouted out. "Where is your old daddy girl?'

"Sir, whose daddy are you talking about? Do you mean Mr. Brown?" Before I allowed him to answer, I was able to interrupt with a follow-up response. "Oh, he is over by the car. By the way, my name is Lauren."

George didn't seem interested in knowing my name. He left our conversation to join Mr. Brown. I panicked as I suddenly remembered I did not have any car insurance which meant I would not be taking my car home. This is terrible. The thought of having to ride back home with Mr. Brown would be a nightmare. There was no way in hell I would be riding back in a car with that nasty man. I would rather hitchhike than be a passenger in his car.

Before I was able to go any further with my thoughts or plans, Mr. George and Mr. Brown informed me that George had agreed to drive the car back to our house that day. Mr. Brown would drive George back to his home later that evening after he joined us for dinner This news was a miracle. I didn't waste any time, as I immediately headed for my car to wait for Mr. George.

# Chapter 25
# You Get What You Pay For

I was spared the embarrassment and funny looks by many of my classmates, as "old Bessie" ran for maybe 4 months before she got towed to the junk yard. In many ways, I felt set-up and taken advantage of. I knew nothing about how to take care of a car and no one bothered to teach me. I knew a car needed gas to run. What I didn't know was a car also needed something called "free-on." This liquid was important for a car to have particularly when the weather turned cold. Sadly, old Bessie never got any "free-on" which led to her trip to the junk yard.

My grandmother would call this kind of situation the "work of the devil." She always believed that the devil worked in "mysterious ways." It remained a mystery as to why the Browns left me to figure out all the ins and outs of taking care of a car. Once the car had been towed out of the yard, it seemed easier to move past this negative memory. One month had passed since the car had been towed and it was almost as if I had forgotten about old Bessie. But that all changed when I came home from school late one afternoon and found a white envelope lying on my bed. There wasn't a strong sense of urgency to open up this envelope. I felt it was another message from Glenda begging me to lie about where she had been over the past two nights. But after I looked back at the envelope, I realized this was a business type envelope, whereas Glenda has always used more animated and playful ones. It was at that time I experienced a funny feeling that something was wrong. The only way to know what was inside was to open the envelope.

After opening up the envelope, I was shocked to find a bill from the towing company. My first reaction was, this must be a joke or a mistake. Once I took a few breaths, I knew I would not be paying this money. The truth about this situation was I never called to request towing services. It became clear to me that the Browns would figure this out. I never received another towing bill, and the subject of the car was never discussed.

As crazy as it may sound, I wanted to believe that after all I went through with old Bessie, the Browns might reach out and offer to help me with my next car. The only reaching out that was offered was to drive me back to the country to look at another "piece of shit." The funny part of their offer was they dropped it and never brought it back up. Maybe the reason for this was they became focused on packing their suitcases for a two-week trip to Hawaii.

Those two weeks without the Browns were just as good, if not better, than getting a different car. Their time being away turned into a vacation for me. I felt a sense of relief not having to face them and not worrying about their agenda. Coming home from school was a joy, as I didn't have to worry about what Mr. Brown had on his mind. The last night before the Brown's return, I spent time with my favorite person, Vu, at his house.

That last night was extra special, as Vu and I snuggled together. We didn't have to think about a curfew or me having to dodge Mr. Brown. It was the first time that Vu kissed me. It had been one of the best nights I had experienced in a long time. This night left me with butterflies and feelings that were new for me. I wondered if I was falling in love. Whatever it was, sure felt good. I arrived home much later than I expected on that particular night. None of this mattered, as I deserved a night of peace and belonging. Upon my return, I received a surprise as I found Glenda home alone.

"Hi. What are you doing home?" I asked.

"Huh, I live here. Did you forget?"

"You know what I mean. I thought you might be asleep or something."

"Yeah, I know. You thought I'd be with Tracy. Well, that ain't going to happen anytime soon. He has done gone and showed his ass."

"What do you mean? What ..."

"I'll tell you. I found out that he has been sleeping with his old slutty ex-girlfriend. He won't be getting anymore of me until he stops sleeping with that honkey tonk hussy."

"Gosh, I'm sorry Glenda. That's awful. Are you O.K?"

"Of course, I'm O.K. If I need a man, I can get one. But enough about me. I want the juicy details on what you and Vu did tonight. Did you and him make it to home base? Was it good? Tell me everything. I want to hear it all and don't leave out any details. It will stay between us. I ain't going to tell anyone."

"Well, to tell you the truth Glenda, my night may not be that exciting to you. But if you really want to hear it. I'll tell you."

"Yes, tell me. I need to hear something good."

"Okay. Well, you know that Vu is kind of shy."

"Stop with the bullshit and get to the point."

"Well, we didn't make it to second base."

"Why not? Now that was a wasted night. Y'all had the whole night alone and that's all y'all did? Well, I'm sorry I don't mean to make you feel bad. It's just that you should have made it to home-base by now. I mean, you are almost going to be a senior in High School."

"Glenda, I'm not in a hurry to get to home-base. I need to be sure that Vu is the right one for me."

"Well, it's your decision. I just want you know that you are missing out on a lot of fun."

I decided to change the subject as Glenda had her mind made up on what she wanted to talk about, and I wasn't interested.

"So, have you heard any word about when your mom and dad are coming home?"

"No, but when they do call, I'll let you know."

"Thanks. I'm pretty tired. I think I will say goodnight. See you tomorrow."

Just as I walked past Glenda, the telephone rang, and she jumped up to answer. I was curious to hear who was calling so late. I never had an opportunity to ask about the telephone call. Within seconds she yelled out, "I'm leaving now. Tracy called. He is picking me up in 10 minutes."

I couldn't believe my ears. Was she really going to see Tracy after how he treated her? This wasn't my problem and she needed to figure it out. I quickly turned my thoughts to having one final peaceful night of sleep. As I reached to turn out the light, I heard a voice calling out my name.

"Are you asleep yet? I need to tell you something. Tracy just called again, and we are definitely back together. He should be here any moment."

Something happened to me, and I snapped. "Are you crazy? Have you totally lost your damn mind? Don't you see what this guy is about?"

'No, I'm not crazy. I know what I'm doing. I will handle him. Don't you get it? He has come back to me. I got what he wants."

"You just don't get it, do you?"

"Get what? What are you talking about?"

"I'm talking about respecting yourself more."

"I do respect myself," she said defiantly.

"O.K. I'm sorry if I've made you mad. I just don't want anything bad to happen to you. I'm going to bed now."

"I'm not mad at you. I know that we are different in these kinds of things. I'm more free spirited and you are more like a 'goodie-two-shoes' kind of girl. Now don't wait for me. I won't be home for a while."

"Don't worry, I'm going to bed. Just make sure you have your key."

Falling asleep that night was interrupted with thoughts of how desperate Glenda was. I wasn't sure which was worse, pathetic Glenda or the horrible Browns. Those depressing thoughts kept me awake. The clock showed the time of 2:00 a.m. yet I was still wide awake.

I pulled out a book to read hoping it would help me fall asleep. After reading only a few chapters, I began to hear my stomach growling and decided I needed to have a snack. The thought of raiding the refrigerator seemed exciting, as this was not allowed by the Browns. There were rules to follow once the kitchen was closed and tonight I was going to break that rule and would help myself to whatever I wanted. I joyfully skipped down the hallway and was surprised to find a light in Glenda's bedroom. Could Glenda have left this light on before she left to go out? No, I knew that I didn't see this light when I came down the hall to go to bed. Should I just go into the room? Before I could think any further. There were sounds inside.

"Glenda, are you in there?"

"Yes, I am."

"Can I come in?"

"No, I don't feel like talking. Tracy never came to get me tonight. Isn't that what you really want to know? I need to go to bed now."

"Sure. I understand. I'm really sorry. If you need to talk, you can come to my room. I had been down that lonely road many times and knew how it felt to be left alone. No one deserves to be treated like that."

There was no answer back. I decided it was best for me to leave Glenda alone with her thoughts. It was hard for me to walk away and to leave her in that state of pain.

# Chapter 26
# The End is in Sight

The Browns' trip to Hawaii seemed to be the topic of discussion for months around the household. These conversations were always narrated by Mrs. Brown, as she made sure everyone in the entire town knew that she had been kissed by Don Ho at a Hawaiian Luau. There were never any photos shared from their trip, a fact I always found to be unusual. There had been many times when I wondered if Mrs. Brown had actually made up the story of being kissed by this supposed famous Island man in Hawaii.

After about 3 months of hearing this same old boring story being told, I slipped up and blurted out and confronted Mrs. Brown about not having any pictures. "I just can't believe that you don't have any pictures. I mean after all that excitement and having such a famous man give you a smacker of a kiss, you didn't get a picture?"

Mrs. Brown shot back, "What is it about this picture? Why are you and everyone else so caught up in wanting to see a picture? It almost sounds like y'all don't believe the man kissed me. Look, the kiss was special enough, or should I say, it was the real deal, and a picture wasn't necessary."

For a brief moment it came to me that those were the kind of words that I expected and often heard coming out of Glenda's mouth rather than Mrs. Brown. I found it hard to bear another second being in the same room with that woman and knew that if I stayed any longer, I would say something I would regret.

However, I did not leave, as Glenda had appeared out of nowhere and blocked my way out of the room. The thought of leaving the room quickly escaped me when I saw Glenda waving several black and white photos. It only took a few blinks to see that these pictures were of Mrs. and Mr. Brown on a beach that was surrounded by tall palm trees. Before I was able to reach down for the pictures, I heard Glenda speak.

"I couldn't wait, Mom, I had to open them. Don't be mad. I wanted to see what Hawaii really looked like. Look, Mom, where's the picture of you and that Island guy. You, know, the guy that kissed you."

Mrs. Brown shot back, "Glenda Ann, I told you about opening up mail. Give me those pictures now. I can't believe that you opened my mail again. Did you know that opening others' mail is a crime? Now don't ever do it again. You understand me?"

All I could think was *Wow, she did lie about having her picture made after all. Poor old soul. She should be kissing her old desperate husband who really wants to kiss her. I really don't feel sorry for her at all. She shouldn't be lying in the first place.*

Mrs. Brown had a hard time calming down that day and it was really Mr. Brown that brought things to a halt when he came into the room.

"What is going on?" he asked.

"You need to talk to your daughter. She has been opening up my mail."

Before Mr. Brown was able to respond, she continued her rant. "Yeah, only one roll of our pictures came from the trip. The most important roll hasn't arrived. The roll that shows me and Mr. Ho."

I waited to hear Mr. Brown's response; however, one never came. Rather, the afternoon ended with tension as Mr. Brown made a quiet exit from the room and remained silent about Mrs. Browns story. There was never any more discussion surrounding the vacation photos and it remained a mystery if the second roll of pictures ever arrived.

Beyond the family drama, in the final year of my life living with the Browns I had multiple personal successes. This increased my optimism, confidence, and determination to embrace a life that had been taken away from me. My senior year is when these opportunities for success truly unfolded.

My last school year was unique, and I think it was mostly because I aimed high for academic achievement. And for once, I experienced what it felt like for someone to respect and believe in me. My interest and involvement with the newspaper staff that began in my sophomore year continued into my junior year. I had no plans on how I would proceed with working on the newspaper during my senior year, if at all. This all changed, when I was given the opportunity to be the editor-in-chief for "The Fledgling" newspaper. This was huge. I walked around for days feeling as if I had been promoted to "commander-in-chief." I felt important.

I had no desire or intentions of sharing this amazing news with the Browns, as I knew they would just blow it off. These plans eventually had to change, when I learned that I would be recognized in the local newspaper for my successes at the end of the year. I would be recognized in the local newspaper for receiving an award for my editorial stories with the school newspaper. I knew that Mrs. Brown always started off her day with a cup of coffee and the local newspaper, as if she wasn't nosey enough. I knew that the chances of Mrs. Brown missing this article would be slim to none.

Another event that was linked to my editor-in-chief award involved an invitation to the end-of-year awards banquet for seniors. Over the years, this event had been widely advertised among other seniors and family members. The last surprise that I needed, or wanted, was to have the Browns take credit for any of my school accomplishments.

During my senior year, I was also on the school's gymnastic team. The gymnastic team had several school performances, during which I was featured as a solo act on the balance beam. My interest in gymnastics began as a modest curiosity from personal interest but progressed into higher levels of accomplishment. I received praise and support from both students and teachers for my performances.

I spent less and less time being around the Browns during the final months of my senior year. Much of this was related to being fully involved in school activities. For once in my life, I experienced fun and received recognition for my hard work.

The grand finale of my final school year was inviting Vu to the Senior Prom. I knew that this decision would be risky, as Vu didn't like being in the spotlight. This was my last and only chance to go to a prom, as I missed out on last year's prom. For many students, the senior prom was the last big social event that would bring about memories for a lifetime.

I wasn't sure about my strategy for asking Vu to the prom. He may not completely understand what the prom is all about. However, I was sure he would trust me and accept my invitation. The biggest challenge surrounding the prom for both Vu and me would be money. How would we pay for the fancy clothes and the restaurant? Another popular ritual related to prom was renting a limousine for the night. This would be totally out of the question for Vu and me. Somehow, we would figure out the transportation. That would be the least of my worries.

With the prom only two weeks away, it was essential that I pop the question, asking Vu to be my date. It was a big relief that Vu accepted my invitation and at the same time he was curious and excited about the events surrounding the prom.

I felt the need to buy our tickets for the prom particularly since I invited Vu. One week before the prom, it hit me that Vu and I would be on our own for my gown and his tuxedo.

In the back of my mind, I wondered if the Browns would offer to pitch in with my dress. It was no surprise that nothing was ever mentioned about the prom. I knew I had to think quickly, as time was running out. Well, to my surprise, I received a call from Vu with some exciting information. He shared that his aunt was a seamstress and wanted to make a dress for me to wear to the prom.

However, this would be no ordinary dress, this would be an ornate Vietnamese dress, called an "Ao Dai." I was thrilled and honored that Vu's aunt wanted to make a dress for me. With all the excitement about the dress, I stopped to think about what exactly will my dress, the Ao Dai, look like? I didn't have to think about this for very long, as Vu surprised me with a photo of his mother wearing one. The dress that his mother was wearing in the photo was magical. It was layered with rhinestones and lace. Becoming all wrapped up in how beautiful the dress was, it struck me that we still needed to get a tuxedo for Vu. I was determined to have a plan for getting him a tuxedo. In the meantime, I was left with the thought of me walking out into the living room, dressed in my Ao Dai, and asking Mrs. Brown, how she liked my prom dress?

# Chapter 27
# Things are Looking Up

My senior year was the best year of my life living at the Browns. Yet it seemed to come and go way too fast. My grandmother had always said, "All good things will come to an end." Well, living at the Browns had never been fun or exciting, rather, it felt like an eternity with no visible ending in sight. There were many days that I daydreamed about what life would be like outside, away from the doom and gloom of living in what felt more like a dungeon than a home.

The only place where I truly felt connected was in school. This was a place I was validated by teachers who believed in me. There was one special teacher that made the greatest difference in my high school achievement and success. This was Mrs. Capps, who taught Journalism. She was also the instructor for the high school newspaper class. My three years of journalism classes under the instruction of Mrs. Capps led to a unique and emotional relationship that at times created challenges for her role of teacher and me as student. She and I seemed to always be on the same page, yet I still knew I was a student, and she was the teacher. This relationship between me and Ms. Capp never really strayed off course as we maintained boundaries.

However, on one occasion we did go to a more personal space in this mentoring relationship. The school newspaper was scheduled to print its last edition for the school year, yet it had never occurred to me that I would be writing my final editor's column.

"So, what do you have planned for your final editorial?" She asked.

"What do you mean?"

"You do realize this will be your last edition for the year," she explained.

"Well to be honest with you, I've tried to not think about it. I don't do well with goodbyes."

"You must have some ideas about your farewell column?"

"No, Ma'am. I haven't really given it much thought."

She continued her questions. "This truly comes to me as a surprise. Is there anything I can do to help?"

"No Ma'am. I guess I need to pull my myself together and accept that this will be my last column. It seems that time has gone by so fast. I guess, I'm going to miss you, Mrs. Capps." Emotions flowed over me, sadness and more.

I finally found my voice and asked, "Will I ever get to see you again? I don't do well with separation. You have become someone that I can trust. You make me feel like I'm worth something."

To my surprise, she seemed to understand. "Okay. Time-out. Let me have a turn to talk. I have had many students come back to visit me after graduation. Most students come back for a visit during their breaks from college." She paused for just a moment, then asked me another question. "You are going on to college, right?"

I didn't answer immediately, all I could think of was *Oh, great, now I have to tell the truth. I will probably disappoint her.*

She continued, "So, which universities did you apply to?" I remember you talked about medicine and teaching. I know that you can be or do anything you set your mind to. You are a very smart young lady."

"Ms. Capps, I'm so sorry to admit that I didn't apply to any universities." Before I continued to say any more, I paused for her reactions.

"Honey, there is no need to apologize. Everyone has their own path. There are many different ways to go about getting further education."

"So, you are not upset with me?"

"Of course not. I know that you are capable and will accomplish your goals."

"Well, I have decided to enroll in the community college and possibly sign-up for their dental hygiene program. This will be something that I can do short-term that will allow me to become independent and pay my bills. But, Mrs. Capps, don't worry, I will go back later on to get a real degree. That, I promise you."

"Lauren, you have accomplished so much in the last three years, and I am so proud of you." Her smile let me relax. It was such a relief that I wasn't a disappointment in her eyes. She asked the question again. "So, any thoughts on what to write for your last editorial column?"

"No Ma'am, but I will go home and give great thought about it. I will discuss it with you tomorrow."

"That sounds like a good plan. Oh, by the way, are you going to the prom this year?"

"Yep, and I'm so excited too. I missed going last year."

With a little smile, she surprised me again, "I bet I know who you are going with."

We both knew who she was talking about. "Yes, Ma'am, you do know him."

"Well, he is one lucky guy to have a girl as special as you."

She wasn't done surprising me. "Oh, by the way Lauren, I would like to pay for a small ad for the final copy of our newspaper."

Without thinking, I blurted out, "Why would you want to do that? Yes, Ma'am if that's want you really want to do. How large of an ad would you like?"

"I'm thinking of a quarter page size. This size would be plenty for the story that I intend to write."

"Oh, you are going to write a story?" My curiosity grew.

"Yes. It's actually going to be an end of the year summary and final wrap-up on the progress and successes of our newspaper."

"O.K. that sounds like a great idea. I need you to get your copy written by tomorrow. We need to submit all documents for proofing."

"I'll get it written up by tonight. But I am going to drop off the story first thing in the morning at the printer, as this is a special story that I want everyone to read when the paper is hot off the press."

I thought to myself ok this has never been done before, and I was puzzled about what this story would be about. "Well, sure, that should be O.K. I'll reserve the appropriate space for your story."

"O.K. we both should get going, because we have stories to write."

"Yes, Ma'am. Oh, speaking of deadlines and things to do, I have to go and try on my prom dress."

"That sounds like fun. Where did you buy it?"

"Actually, I am having my prom dress professionally designed and made for me."

"That sounds like royalty."

"You have no idea. You will just have to wait and see. Just like I will have to wait and read your news article."

"Sounds like a fair deal to me."

There were times when I could not imagine life without Mrs. Capps being a part of it. Somehow, I managed to convince myself that no matter what, she would always be a part of my life.

Vu was pretty much my transportation for the remainder of my senior year except for a few times I hitched a ride with Glenda. The day that I was to try on my prom dress, Vu had agreed to take me. His aunt spoke no English and I was certainly not proficient in Vietnamese. During the time that I tutored Vu, I took the opportunity to read up on the Vietnamese culture and family lifestyles and learned a great deal about their family values and traditions. This learning opportunity truly paid off. I chose to show my respect to Vu's aunt by taking her a small gift on the day I tried on my prom dress. I had no idea that my prom dress would be perfectly tailored and ready for me to take home on that day.

Vu never talked about the talent of his people, as he would often refer to them. However, he did on occasion boast or brag about their cooking and tailoring talents, as being top notch. I felt and looked like a goddess queen on that day, when I saw myself in the mirror with this long, oriental red dress embellished with designs of dragons, shiny sequins, stars, and lightning bolts.

With the excitement of the dress, the prom and Mrs. Capps's mystery newspaper article, I completely forgot about how I would come up with a plan to get the dress into the house without anyone seeing it. I had to think fast. Nothing was coming to mind. But my worry was unfounded. No one was home when Vu dropped me off. Mission accomplished.

The newspaper went to press for final publication and the mystery article written by Mrs. Capps was revealed. The newspapers had been delivered as a courtesy by the local printers. Mrs. Capps called me out of English class once the papers were delivered to our school.

As I approached Mrs. Capps's classroom, it dawned on me that she would be teaching a class. But my curiosity and excitement of the mysterious news article got the best of me, so I reached out my hand to knock on the door. Her classroom door opened, and I was face-to-face with Mrs. Capps and the newspaper. She quickly stepped outside in the hallway and said she was leaving the class with a student teacher. We went to the library to look over the newspaper.

Once we were settled in one of the private areas of the library, Mrs. Capps's opened the newspaper to her article and handed it to me, and said, "I wanted you to be the first person to see this."

Mrs. Capps had written an article that basically stated that she had dedicated the year's final edition of the newspaper to me, and also acknowledged me as the recipient of the "Editor-in-Chief Award."

I was stunned. It took me a minute to say what I really thought, "Wow, I'm so surprised that you would do such a thing for me. You are the only person who has done anything like this for me."

"Lauren, you have done all the work. You deserve all the credit. Now, it's time for everyone to know."

Without even giving it any thought, I jumped up and went over to hug Mrs. Capps. She hugged me back and added, "Now let's go sell some newspapers. You are famous." We both laughed.

"Oh, Lauren, don't forget about tomorrow night. It's the awards banquet."

"Yes, Ma'am. I will definitely be there. Will you be there?"

"I wouldn't miss it for the world."

The rest of that day at school you would have thought I was the most important person in the world. People would stop me in the hallway and say "congratulations" or "way to go, chief." I was asked by one person if I would autograph their newspaper. It took until the end of the day for most of the newspaper excitement to dwindle down.

But everything was not great. I knew deep down what was ahead of me in my decision to invite or not invite Mrs. Brown to the awards banquet. I put off making any decision until I could think it over. It turns out I didn't have to make this decision after all. Glenda had purchased a copy of the school newspaper and left it on the kitchen table; somehow Mrs. Brown took the time out of her busy life to read it. It surprised me when Mrs. Brown asked me about my going to the Awards Banquet.

Without any warmth or enthusiasm in her voice, she asked, "So, do you know what this school awards banquet is all about? Did someone nominate you for an award?"

I thought silently, *you dumb witch, of course I know.*

I managed to be passably polite and said, "Uh, yeah… I'm the Editor-in-Chief of the school newspaper and I've been selected to receive a recognition award. Do you have any more questions?" There was silence, as Mrs. Brown did not respond.

I decided to break the silence by asking again, "Is there anything else you'd like to know about the Awards Banquet? You can always knock on my door if you want any more details of my event." With still no reply, I turned away and started to walk towards my bedroom." Before I reached for the doorknob to my bedroom, I heard Mrs. Brown voice and turned around."

"Well, yes, I guess I'd like to know the date and time of the banquet?"

*My God woman can't you read? The article that you just supposedly read has all that dang information.*

I struggled to stay polite, "Well, yes, all that information is in the newspaper that's right in front of you. But anyway, its tomorrow night at 7:00 p.m."

"O.K. Well, I'll go. What time should I be ready?"

*God, this woman has really lost her mind.* "Well, we should probably leave around 6:30. I told Vu to be here around 6:20."

"Vu? What does he have to do with this banquet?"

"Well to start with, Vu is my boyfriend. He is going with me to the banquet."

"How are y'all getting there?"

"What do you mean?"

"Is he driving his car?"

"Well, he does have a car. Would you like to drive?"

There was silence and moments of awkwardness before she answered, "Well, I'm not sure about that. I mean it might be best if your boyfriend drives his own car. I tell you what, maybe I could just ride with y'all."

"What? You want to ride with us?"

"Why not?"

"I'm just surprised. I mean Vu's car is not really that nice. You have such a nicer, fancier car than he does. Also, his car smells a lot like smoke because his dad smokes in the car when he drives."

"Well, that's O.K. I can always put the window down. "

"I'm sure Vu will not mind if you want to ride with us. He is a nice guy."

"That sounds good. I will be ready at 6:30."

I left our conversation feeling confused at first but later on that night, I figured it all out. It really began to make sense. Mrs. Brown really didn't want Vu to be in her car.

The more I thought about Mrs. Brown and her motives, the angrier I felt. I suddenly felt confused about her even being a part of my success and coming to the banquet. Perhaps I should not include her after all. I fell asleep that night tormented by not knowing what to do.

# Chapter 28
# No Looking Back

It seemed like last year living at the Browns was going by so fast. I woke up one Friday morning and realized that I would be going to my very first prom in a little over 24 hours. Then another thought quickly popped into my mind that today I would also pick up my beautiful prom dress and bring it home. It knew it would be important to sneak the dress into the house without drawing any attention. I didn't want anything to mess up my plans to be the center of attention and dare I say, create a bit of disturbance around the old homestead.

Hum…as some folks used to say, "What goes around, comes around." All I can say is "ready or not, here I come." I thought to myself, what a moment that would be when Mrs. Brown saw me in my beautiful Ao Dai. I felt a rush of excitement course through my body and wanted the moment to happen right away. However, I reminded myself all great things in life are worth waiting for. This distraction almost made me late for my ride to school. I somehow managed to make up the lost time and was outside five minutes before Vu drove into the driveway to get me to school.

That particular morning, Vu seemed more cheerful than most early mornings. I wondered what he had on this mind. I knew the only way to find out would be to ask him.

"So, what's got you all happy this morning?"

"I don't know," he said unconvincingly.

"Come on. You can tell me."

"It's a surprise."

"A surprise for me?"

"I can't tell you right now."

"When can you tell me?" My curiosity grew.

"You will know tomorrow night at the prom."

"You mean I have to wait until then?"

"Yep," he said, holding steady with his refusal to tell me.

It became pretty clear that Vu had no plans to change his mind about letting his secret out of the bag that morning. He did, however, remind me about his plans to take me to get my prom dress that afternoon after school. The rest of the day at school felt like an eternity. The excitement and anticipation of the prom had both girls and guys lost in their own world, as girls bragged about their dresses and guys tried to downplay what they planned to wear.

It was during the passing of one of these conversations, that I realized Vu still didn't have a tuxedo. I began to feel guilty and selfish for being so wrapped up in my attire while ignoring or forgetting about Vu.

I knew I had to calm down and think this out. It didn't take long before I had the answer. The only answer would be to take money from my savings account and help Vu rent a tuxedo. I knew I would have to go about this in a cautious way, so as not to take charge ignoring what Vu wanted to do.

Before I was able to beat myself up any further, I heard my name called out. It was only after three school buses left the front of the school, that I saw Vu in his father's car waiting for me.

"Come on Lauren, let's go. We're going to be late."

"What do you mean? I thought we were supposed to pick up the dress at 4:00."

"Don't worry, we are going to get your dress but there's also something else I need to get before five o'clock today."

"O.K. Are you going to tell me what this secret is?" Although I was really curious, this was a surprise that I looked forward to. I decided to keep up the pressure in a lighthearted way.

"Huh, no. You have to wait until tomorrow night." He had a teasing quality to his reply.

"Oh, so you are playing that kind of game?" I kept the moment going.

"No, this is not a game. This is my word."

At that point I figured it was time to leave it alone.

My prom dress turned out to be far more beautiful than I had ever imagined it could be. I never understood why Vu's aunt took such an interest in me and went to all the trouble and expense to make me a prom dress. The only clue that made sense came the day when I learned from

Vu that his aunt had given me a real compliment. She said to him that I "was different from most American girls and that it was safe to be around me." Vu assured me his aunt didn't take kindly to American girls and that she had decided to give me a chance. I later learned that this aunt's husband left her for an American woman once they arrived from Vietnam which caused her to dislike and not trust most American girls.

After picking up my dress and thanking Vu's aunt, I knew the next hurdle was to sneak my dress into the Browns' home. Things all worked out, as no one was home when Vu dropped me off. I stored my dress in the back of my closet making it difficult for anyone to see. The excitement from thoughts of both my beautiful dress and going to the prom made it difficult for me to fall asleep that night. Somehow, I pulled myself away from my prom dress and managed to steal a few hours of sleep.

The day of the big event finally arrived. So much of my attention about the prom had been centered on my dress that I had totally forgotten all about my hair and make-up. I knew that I surely wasn't going to a beauty salon and spend a fortune for one of those beehive hairdos. Neither would I get a make-up do-over that would make me look like some kind of "Jezebel." I knew that Vu had always liked my hair long and pulled back with a clip and he had always preferred very little make-up. That certainly made things easy and saved me money to help Vu pay for the prom pictures and late-night dinner after prom.

I stayed in my room much of the day, as I had no desire to spoil the great mood I was in and certainly running into Mr. Brown would make that happen. I had several things that needed to be done before Vu picked me up. It was both important and necessary that I write a thank you note to Vu's Aunt for making the beautiful prom dress. The other task was to finish reading a library book that was already one week past due. Before I started on my agenda, it dawned on me that the Browns' routine on Saturday morning was to take out Mr. Brown's parents for breakfast and then grocery shopping. What this all boiled down to was having the house to myself for four hours.

I took full advantage of having the house all to myself. This opportunity was rare, and I was determined to enjoy it. I decided to postpone reading my library book and letter writing to Vu's aunt. In place of completing my agenda, I freely allowed myself to raid the refrigerator.

Surprisingly, I found cookies, soda and leftover banana pudding and proceeded to help myself by having a large glass of coke and five cookies. This moment of freedom and peace left me feeling like a queen.

I ended up having the house all to myself for most of the day. The Browns stayed out until 5:00 p.m. A very small part of me wanted to believe that Mrs. Brown would come home with a special surprise for me related to the prom. It was no surprise that Mrs. Brown showed up empty handed.

Shortly after my relaxed afternoon at home, it occurred to me that I had not seen Glenda all day. I'd wondered if she was still going to the prom. And if so, would she be going with Tracy? Glenda and I rarely saw much of each other during our senior year and pretty much drifted apart when we got seriously involved with our boyfriends. The one conversation that I will never forget between Glenda and me was she would someday marry a rich doctor who would take care of her and make sure she had lots of money.

After being distracted, I reminded myself I had more important things to worry about and that Glenda would not be one of those tonight. After separating myself from Glenda and her problems, I continued getting ready and concentrated on the final touches for both Vu and the prom. It was also important for me to be ready once Vu arrived. The last thing that I needed would be to keep him waiting and to risk that he might be confronted with the Browns and their unpredictability.

After having everything in place, I decided to step up to the wall mirror and to admire just how pretty I looked. I also paused and reflected on the generosity of Vu's aunt and her respect for me. After pulling myself away from mirror, I remembered that I had no idea what Vu would be wearing for prom. At the same time, it really didn't matter. What mattered was being with him.

It was about that time I heard a loud knock at the door that called for my attention.

"Yes, who is it?"

"It's Glenda, can I come in?"

*Oh my God, where did she come from?* Having to think fast, I came back with a response.

"Huh, I'm not quite dressed yet. You will have to wait. I didn't know you were home."

"Yeah, I've been out shopping all day for a dress to wear to the prom. I finally found one. Look, Vu is here. So, you better finish getting ready fast. Also, Mom wants to take pictures of us before we leave."

"O.K., I will just meet you in the living room shortly."

*Boy that was a close call. Glenda almost messed up my plans.* The most important thing was about to happen. I was ready to get the show on the road.

Without any further hesitation, I grabbed my purse and made my way down the hallway to show off my beautiful dress. I entered the living room and found myself face-to-face with Mrs. Brown. This was an awkward moment. However, things got much better, once I saw Vu standing in the same room.

The next thing I remember from that moment were sounds of laughter that erupted from Mrs. Brown. There was no reason for me to focus on Mrs. Brown's odd and ridiculous behaviors. It was about that time, Mrs. Brown became more engaged through her curiosity by asking me, "Are you wearing a costume?" She further stated, "I thought you had plans for going to the prom not a "pow wow."

I must say, I was not expecting this kind of reaction from Mrs. Brown. It truly took me by surprise. It was only a few seconds following Mrs. Brown's comments that I felt Vu's arms around my waist, at which time he nudged me closer to him and took charge. I had never seen this side of him, as he stood up for me and addressed Mrs. Brown's confused state of mind. Vu assertively informed her that the dress I was wearing carried a great deal of meaning.

Vu further elaborated and shared the details of my dress. "No, Lauren's prom dress is not a costume dress. Her dress is a special Vietnamese dress called an Ao Dai." Vu continued to educate her on the history of this dress and even surprised me by pulling out from his tuxedo jacket pocket, a piece of paper that had information on the Ao Dai.

Throughout this encounter, Mrs. Brown remained silent and devoid of any emotions. It had been only a moment before Vu continued to inform Mrs. Brown of the history of my dress. The next words that I heard came from Vu. He approached both Mr. and Mrs. Brown by extending and sharing the following, "Good Night, I will have Lauren home by midnight." We did not stall or wait in anticipation of Mr. Brown or Mrs. Brown responding, rather, we turned around and walked towards the door and made our exit.

# Chapter 29
# A Night to Remember

The moment Vu and I escaped the Browns' dungeon to go to the school prom was when our fun and excitement started. On the way to prom, there was no real chit chat between Vu and me about how he took charge and did not back down from Mrs. Brown. If I could have read his mind, I would say that it was obvious that neither one of us wanted to waste our time talking about Mrs. Brown. Instead, we kicked back and cranked up the radio to the music of Jackson Brown, his favorite artist since he arrived in the U.S. Many of our Saturday night dates involved driving around town, listening to the radio along with an occasional stop at the Dairy Queen for a banana split.

The moment had arrived. Vu and I were only steps away from a magical night. Just before our prom tickets were collected at the door, I panicked and said out loud, "Vu, do you know how to dance?" Thinking to myself, *My God, why did I go and stick my foot in my mouth. Why did I say such a stupid thing?*

"Well, I think I do know how to. In Vietnam, I learned how to do many kinds of dances. You will see. I will just show you. I mean I will teach you. You know, like you teach me how to speak English."

It was an enchanting night. Vu and I owned the dance floor. For once in my life, I saw myself as Cinderella at the ball. I was envied by many of my classmates and a few teachers. Another unexpected surprise happened. I was selected with a few of the most popular and beautiful girls to be photographed for the school yearbook. I was convinced that it was the Vietnamese dress that allowed for me to even be considered for such an honor.

At the end of the evening, the D.J. announced the last song was about to be played for everyone to have a final dance. As the prom came to a close, I realized I had not seen any sign of Glenda all night. The last conversation that I had with her involved her plans to sneak away to the beach for the weekend after the prom. My gut told me that Glenda never planned to make it to prom and was beach bound.

With many of my peers crowding the dance floor for the final dance, I turned to Vu and asked if he wanted to make an early exit to avoid a traffic jam out of the school parking lot. In the end, it all worked out as we joined others on the dance floor and still managed to exit the school gym ahead of others. Once we were in Vu's car, we were not bothered by the traffic, as we talked and reminisced about the prom.

It had always been a tradition to eat at a fancy restaurant after the prom. Of course, fancy for some people could have been taco-bell or even Pizza Hut. Vu and I had not discussed or made any real plans for going to a restaurant. The truth was, we were both short on money from our spending on personal items and extra snacks at the prom. Popular people and those who had a lot of money would go to *The Barn*. A part of me wanted to go to Taco Bell, as I knew that Vu didn't have the kind of money it took to eat at *The Barn*.

Out of respect, I decided to let Vu make the decision on where we would go. To my surprise, Vu drove straight to *The Barn*. After we secured a parking space, he exclaimed, "surprise!" I continued to let Vu take the lead, as he seemed excited and determined to end the evening with only the best. We were greeted and escorted to a table for two and given a menu. Before having a chance to open the menu, the waiter returned to our table with a single red rose and a bottle of sparking water.

Everything seemed to be happening so fast. I felt like I was sitting in a castle next to my prince. This moment was interrupted, as Vu asked, "Are you surprised that I brought you here?"

"Yes. I'm also the happiest girl in the world." From that moment, I decided not to ask Vu any questions about money, as he was in charge and seemed happy and proud.

You would have thought we were a "Royal Couple" with no worries in the world. The waiter returned to our table to take our order. It was at that time, we both realized that we had not even opened the menu. To be honest, I was afraid to open the menu. My fear was related to the price and cost of menu items. My fears were lifted when the waiter shared that all menu items had been discounted in honor of the school prom. It was such a relief to hear about the menu pricing. We quickly opened up our menus and selected seafood pasta. The restaurant was full of life and endless energy, as couples were in their own fantasy world. Our dinner also came with a dessert. Before we knew it, couples were starting to leave the restaurant. We managed to linger around and were the last couple to leave. What had been a magical night was coming to an end. This would be a night to remember forever.

Once we were settled back in Vu's car, I was reminded of where Vu was taking me next. Returning to the Browns was the last place I wanted to be. At that moment, I decided that I had to leave the Browns sooner than later. Another decision that I made was to share my plans with Vu. He certainly deserved to know and would understand.

The drive back home was far less chatty and there was a notable silence between the two of us. I wondered if Vu had noticed my quietness and if so, what he might make of it. Would he think I wasn't thankful for the great night that we just had? I had to break the silence and spill the beans about my future plans.

Before I could get any words out, I heard Vu's voice, "Ha, what's on your brain? Why are you so quiet? Are you mad at me? Did I do something wrong tonight?"

"Of course not. You did everything right. Tonight was the best night of my life. I just don't want it to end."

"What does that mean? The night has to end. I mean tomorrow has to come. Then we will have another night. Right? You don't have any power over stopping time."

It became clear that Vu just wasn't getting it. I had to stop him and explain what I felt. He deserved to know my true heart. "O.K. hold on a minute. I need to explain what I'm trying to say. When someone is having a good time with a special person, it's hard to walk away. In some way, you want to hold onto the moment because it may never happen again. Because when you give it up and when it ends, you are afraid it may never happen or come around again."

"Wow, that sounded beautiful. I mean kind of like Mr. Phillips poetry class."

At that moment, I wasn't sure if I should laugh or cry. In the back of my mind, I knew that Vu was still learning American culture. I decided to let it go and enjoy the humor in his comments. Yet, I knew I wanted him to know more and fully understand. I had made up my mind that before he dropped me off at the Browns, he would know the truth.

"Okay. Vu, I have something I really want to talk about. It's not about any poetry. It's about me and us."

"I like it when we talk about us."

"You do? What do you like about it? You have never said anything like that before."

"Well, you ain't never ask me to. But I do tell you sometime, how much I like you."

"Yes, you do. I need you to know that after graduation, I am leaving the Browns."

"Where are you going?"

"I haven't figured that out yet. But I have two months to make a plan. Do you have any suggestions?"

"Yeah, I do. Why don't you come and live with me and my dad?"

Without thinking, I blurted out, "Are you crazy, I can't move in with two men. What would people think of me? I didn't mean it that way. I just don't think that a girl living in a house with two men looks all that good."

"Don't you trust me? Where else would you go? I don't want you to go anywhere else but to stay with me."

"Are you really serious about this? I mean your dad barely knows me. I haven't spent that much time around him. He's so quiet all the time. I really don't know what he thinks about me. Besides, I know how your dad feels about American girls. You have told me yourself that your dad wants you to marry a Vietnamese girl. I know how you feel about me."

"I know my dad don't talk much. It's because he can't speak a lot of English. That's why he is also so quiet. Don't you remember how quiet I was when we first met? Dad has told me that you are different from all those other American girls. You know those girls like Glenda. I have told him how different you are. I even told him how I wished you didn't live with the Browns."

"Wow, your dad really said that? I guess I should believe you because you have never lied to me in the past."

"My kind of people, we don't lie. We take care of our people. We don't leave people and we never put them in those old timer homes that a lot of Americans use to put old people in. In my country that would be a sin and a shame to our people."

In the final minutes before we arrived back at the Browns, I had already made up my mind about leaving their house. However, I decided to wait until I had all the details laid out before I shared them with him. Vu and I were officially ten minutes late getting home from the prom. This would surely mean trouble for me.

Surprisingly, what I found once inside the door was a dark room with no sign of anyone. Still, I wasn't convinced that I would be off the hook for coming home late. I would probably hear about it later the next morning. Somehow, I managed to dodge a bullet and didn't have to face the Browns that night. On the other hand, they were the ones that dodged the bullet and didn't have to face me. After Vu and I said goodnight, I quickly made my way to my bedroom. I had no trouble falling asleep. I was exhausted from my magical night.

Several weeks passed and the Browns never asked me about the prom. The last two months at the Browns were focused on planning my high school graduation. During this same time, I struggled with figuring out the exact details for my departure. Vu continued to try to convince me that living with him and his father was safe and the best plan. I knew that my choices were limited and that I could trust Vu. With only two weeks away from graduation, I was still unsure about where I would live once I left. However, things started to happen that gave me hope.

Vu invited me to have dinner with him and his father at their home. I accepted the invitation but was cautious and uncertain about this.

The dinner turned out to be much more than discussing my pending "homeless" situation, it also involved having my first authentic Vietnamese meal and watching a Vietnamese movie.

Vu and I had not discussed any specific plans on how the topic of my living with him and his father would play out. I suppose I knew it would be handled appropriately by Vu and I knew I could trust him. It clearly seemed to have played out that way. As the movie ended, Vu abruptly began a conversation in Vietnamese with his father that seemed to last forever.

This conversation eventually turned back to include me. Vu explained that he had shared with his father the details about me coming to live with them. I was hopeful that Vu's conversation with his dad was genuine. The best part of the evening happened at the time when we said our good-byes. I turned to give Vu's father one last wave good-bye and was surprised to find a smile that gave me the "green light" that everything was going to okay.

The following night, I made a decision that I would leave exactly one month and 7 days following graduation. Graduation was scheduled on June 7, 1979, at which time I would still be 17 years old and not a legal adult.

There had been an agreement in the foster care paperwork that said I would remain in the legal custody of the Browns until I turned 18 years old. I was determined to not let any of that legal crap come between my happiness and excitement. I certainly would not allow it to change my personal decision to leave on 7/14/1979.

It took only a few seconds after I had made peace with my departure details that I realized the date I chose was on my 18th birthday. Wow, now that would be the best birthday celebration and gift I could ever receive.

# Chapter 30
# It's Time for Me to Go

I must have floated on cloud nine for weeks after the prom. Unlike the many things in my life that have been taken away, the memories from the prom would stay with me forever. Old and painful past memories may exceed the few happy ones, but I will always remain hopeful and optimistic that my life ahead will bring opportunities for joy and peace.

The special dress that I wore on the night of the prom will be forever treasured and protected. The thought of losing this dress would be overwhelming. In many ways, this special dress is symbolic and reminds me of royalty.

The more I thought about my dress, the more I started having bad thoughts about what if something happened to it. These thoughts continued to grow into worry. I decided to search and think about an alternative place for storing my dress. The place that I decided on was under my bed with the boxes of shoes and books that were already there.

Securing a spot for storing my dress gave me peace of mind. It also allowed me to focus on my upcoming high school graduation. School continued to be my "happy place" for the last two months living at the Browns. The buzz around school was all about who got accepted into what college and who dumped his/her boyfriend/girlfriend.

I avoided these conversations, as I knew my plans for college had temporarily changed. The priority for me focused on leaving the Browns right after graduation. There were two out-of-state colleges that had accepted my application for enrollment. The timing and circumstances of my life interrupted these offers. My academic and college advisor, Mrs. Finley had no idea I had made this decision until the last week of school. These academic decisions led to a private meeting with my advisor. The meeting was awkward and uncomfortable. My advisor, Mrs. Finley, was curious and surprised about my future academic plans. In many ways, I felt like I disappointed her. My advisor ended our meeting by telling me it's never too late to change directions or choose a different journey. She assured me that I was capable and deserving of any and all things in life.

After leaving Mrs. Finley's office that afternoon, I realized that graduation was only two days ahead. It was also at that time I remembered I had forgotten to pick up my cap and gown for graduation. Once I had picked up my graduation essentials the reality of my future, without the Brown's, was only a few steps away.

Vu and I had made the decision to drive on our own to the graduation ceremony. This decision came after Vu's dad offered to take us out to lunch to celebrate our accomplishments. We would also use this time to finalize the plans for me to move in.

My plans to ride with Vu to graduation had never been discussed with the Browns. At the same time, the Browns never reached out to ask how I would be getting to graduation. The morning of graduation, the Browns were nowhere in sight. This was yet another sign that my life was ready for a new direction with new people.

The graduation ceremony was nothing special and was over before I knew it. I was proud of myself for this accomplishment, despite the many struggles and disappointment I had experienced over the past several years.

Before I had a chance to think any more about these thoughts, I was startled, as I caught a glimpse of Mrs. Brown making her way towards Vu and me. It was at that time, I quickly turned to Vu and asked, "Is there any reason for us to linger?"

"Not for me, I am ready to go. You are my boss. Let's go and have some fun. We just graduated."

"Great, let's get out of here. Don't forget about our plans. Remember, we are picking up your dad for lunch?"

"Of course, I remember. Now, let's go and eat some good food."

"Yes, I'm ready for a burger and fries. I am still a little nervous about finalizing the plan for me to move in."

"Now, you have to relax and trust me. I will not let you down."

I decided it was safe to relax, as Vu had never lied to me and had always been there for me.

The day before graduation, I made a last-minute decision to withdraw all the money from my savings account. I saw no reason to keep an account open that had Mrs. Brown's name on it. The amount of money that was in my savings account totaled $725.00. I had planned on offering $500.00 of this money to Vu's father as a contribution for allowing me to live with them.

I decided to keep this decision to myself, as I knew that Vu would try and talk me out of giving money to his father. I didn't feel good about keeping this from Vu, but I knew in the end, he would understand.

The plan to eat out with Vu's dad changed that day, as he surprised us with a home-cooked Vietnamese meal. Both the meal and the conversation could not have gone better. Vu and his father communicated mostly in Vietnamese. I managed to look interested and pay attention throughout their conversation.

Eventually, their communication ended and then Vu spoke directly to me.

"My dad said he likes you because he knows how much I like you. He also believes you are a good girl. He believes you care about me. The last thing he said to me was, you can move in with us anytime."

"Really? He said that? Are you sure he really means it?"

"Yes, I'm not lying to you."

"Wow, I'm so happy. Can you tell him I said, "Thank you?""

"No, you can tell him."

"Should I tell him in English?"

"Well, do you know how to speak Vietnamese?"

"Of course, I don't."

"O.K. You are going to learn right now how to say, 'Thank you' in our language."

"I am? How is that?"

"Just repeat after me. Cam ung."

"O.K. I will try. Here it goes. Cam ung."

Both Vu and his dad started clapping their hands as signs of their approval.

I pulled out an envelope that had the $500.00 and handed it over to Vu's Dad. He looked confused yet proceeded to open it and then handed the money back to me with a smile. He then turned to Vu and repeated a few words in Vietnamese.

"My Dad is honored that you would want to give him money. But he can't take it. He said that you can come live here without paying him any money."

A big part of me expected Vu's dad to take the money because I knew he didn't have very much to begin with. His decision to turn down the money caught me by surprise. I was unsure about what to say. It was only a matter of seconds before Vu rescued me, moving quickly to our plans for my move-in date.

"So, I told my dad about your birthday, and he suggested that you consider moving in on your birthday. He also knows all about you needing to be 18 years old before you can leave the Browns. My dad does not want any problems from the Browns and wanted to do the right thing about the rules for your age. Oh, my dad said that the only rules that you would have to follow is to stay in school and help out around the house."

"I'll have no problem following those rules. I feel like your dad should expect more from me. It almost seems like he is getting the short end of the stick."

It became clear to me on that day that Vu's dad was a kind, gentle soul who could be trusted. I knew deep down he was not out to take advantage of me. After leaving Vu's house that day, I felt a sense of peace, as I knew living at the Browns was finally coming to an end.

While I felt relieved and excited about my plans to leave the Browns, I still felt anxious that something would go wrong. Right after graduation, I had approximately two weeks before I would permanently move in with Vu and his father.

Those last two weeks at the Browns went by rather quickly. I decided to tell them about my plans for leaving on the day of my official departure. My original plan was to openly discuss my plans for leaving.

This all changed when Mr. Brown approached me trying to play the "tickle game" with me. I was furious and turned him down with a few choice words.

"Listen up you old geezer. Don't you know that 'dirty-old men' never win in the end? So, just give it -up. I am not a fool. You need to go tickle someone who is a heck of a lot older than me. Like maybe your wife! Go figure. Better yet, grow up old man!"

It was after this run-in with Mr. Brown that I decided it would be best to break the news about my leaving on the day of. Otherwise, I would be in a heck of a lot of trouble with Mr. Brown trying to do who knows what to me.

On the eve of my departure, I had anticipated discussion about what plans I had for celebrating my 18th birthday. A household ritual since I had lived at the Browns was putting in your request for your favorite birthday cake and ice cream.

Mrs. Brown never approached me about my choice for a birthday cake. The truth was, it worked out for the best, as I had no plans for hanging around to celebrate my 18th birthday with them. My plans for my birthday far exceeded a birthday cake and ice cream.

On July 14th, 1979, I turned 18 years old. I decided that it would best to ignore the missing birthday cake. I knew that my future and new life was much more important than a birthday cake. I can always get a cake. Having a second chance for a better life doesn't come around very often.

I had packed the majority of personal items over the past two weeks, and gradually moved items to Vu's home. I slept in on my birthday, as I knew Vu would be picking me up mid-afternoon on that day. The final plan for telling the Browns about my leaving would include Vu.

In less than an hour, I expected Vu to arrive and this whole nightmare would be over. My plans seemed to have all worked out with no surprises or traps. Rather it appeared so, until I heard Mrs. Brown's voice off in the distance to Mr. Brown.

"Hey William, I'm going out for a few hours. I don't know exactly when I'll be back. You should go and eat lunch with your mom and dad or make do with leftovers."

"Take your time, I'll be here around the house puttering around. Uh, isn't today Lauren's birthday?"

"What? Who's birthday?"

"Lauren's. Isn't her birthday on July 14th?"

"Darn, I think you're right. I guess it just slipped my mind. William, can you do something for the girl? I've got to get these errands done for the Eastern Star."

"Of course, honey, I'd be glad to celebrate her birthday. Now, you just go on about your business and don't worry about anything."

Thinking to myself: *To hell with that. Dirty old man, you'd be the last person on this earth I'd celebrate my birthday with.* Before I got too carried away and caught up in my anger, I realized I had to stop Mrs. Brown before she left the house. I knew this would be my only chance to tell her. *Dang, I wish Vu were here early.*

I immediately left my bedroom to find Mrs. Brown before she rushed off to her errands. About that time, I heard a loud muffler heralding Vu's car coming up the drive. Thank you, God, for the timing of all this.

"Mrs. Brown, I need to talk to you about something important."

"I'm in a hurry. Can it wait until this afternoon?"

"No, it can't wait. You need to hear this."

At that moment Vu walked up the porch and stood silently behind me as I spoke. "Mrs. Brown, today I'm moving out. I'm leaving here. I'm no longer going to be living here with you and Mr. Brown. I am 18 years old now and feel it's high time for me to make my own decisions."

"Where are you going?"

"I'm going to live with Vu and his family. They have accepted me and are excited about me joining their family. I am happy about my new home. Thank you for giving me a place to live."

Mr. Brown peaked around the corner and said, "Well, we know that today is your birthday."

"Yep, it is. I have already made plans for my birthday and the celebration will start the moment I leave here. Mrs. Brown, I hope you didn't go to any trouble with baking me a birthday cake. If you did, please enjoy it with your family. Well, Vu, let's get this show on the road. Let's go home, we have a lot of celebrating to catch up on."

As we left, my main thoughts were about celebrating my freedom, and my future with Vu, but other hopes and dreams broke through. Key among them were about my four brothers. The foster care system had made no effort to keep me connected with them. Now, as an adult, I had the power to seek them out, and do something about this injustice.

www.ingramcontent.com/pod-product-compliance
Lightning Source LLC
Chambersburg PA
CBHW050526160726
48003CB00001B/482